SINGAPORE BU(

A Guide to Must-See Attractions and

Hidden Gems for Every Traveler

Journeyroots Guide

DISCLAIMER

This guidebook is designed to provide helpful information and insider tips to enhance your travel experience. Every effort has been made to ensure that the information is accurate and up-to-date at the time of publication. However, location changes, prices, hours of operation, and other details may occur after publication, and the author cannot be held responsible for any discrepancies.

This book offers suggestions and recommendations based on research and personal experiences, but it should not be considered a complete or exhaustive resource. Travelers are encouraged to verify information independently, especially regarding safety guidelines, local customs, travel restrictions, and any other important factors related to their trip.

The author disclaims any liability for damages or losses arising from following the advice or recommendations in this guidebook.

All opinions and recommendations are subjective and should be considered as one of many resources available to travelers. Always use your judgment and make informed decisions during your trip.

Travelers should consult the appropriate professionals or authorities before and during their visit for legal, medical, or safety concerns.

Copyright © 2024 by Journeyroots Guide.
All rights reserved.

No part of this book may be reproduced, distributed, or transmitted in any form or by any means, including photocopying, recording, or other electronic or mechanical methods, without the prior written permission of the publisher, except in the case of brief quotations embodied in critical reviews and certain other non-commercial uses permitted by copyright law.

TABLE OF CONTENTS

DISCLAIMER.. 1

INTRODUCTION.. 8

WHY YOU OUGHT TO VISIT SINGAPORE........ 15

10 TIPS ON HOW TO USE THIS GUIDE............... 24

CHAPTER 1: HISTORY... 29

CHAPTER 2: BEST TIME TO VISIT...................... 38
    PACKING THE RIGHT TRAVEL ESSENTIALS 47
    PHRASES TOURIST SHOULD KNOW FOR
    EASY COMMUNICATION.................................. 63

CHAPTER 3: HOW TO ARRIVE............................ 68

CHAPTER 4: GETTING AROUND........................ 76

CHAPTER 5: OPTIONS FOR ACCOMMODATION 83

CHAPTER 6: MUST-SEE ATTRACTIONS............ 90

CHAPTER 7: HIDDEN GEMS.................................98

CHAPTER 8: MUST DO HIKES AND TRAILS.. 105

CHAPTER 9: BUCKET LIST FOR SOLO TRAVELERS............ 112

CHAPTER 10: BUCKET LIST FOR COUPLES.. 121

CHAPTER 11: BUCKET LIST FOR FAMILY WITH KIDS............ 129

CHAPTER 12: BUCKET LIST FOR GROUP...... 137

CHAPTER 13: BUCKET LIST FOR ADVENTURE SEEKERS............ 144

CHAPTER 14: TOP RESTAURANT............ 150
- Budget Travelers............ 150
- Family with Kids Travelers............ 152
- Luxury Travelers............ 153
- Solo Travelers............ 155
- Vegetarian and Vegan Travelers............ 156

CHAPTER 15: WHERE TO TAKE PHOTOGRAPHS FOR MEMORIES............ 159

CHAPTER 16: SHOPPING AND SOUVENIRS... 164

CHAPTER 17: NIGHTLIFE AND ENTERTAINMENT............ 171

CHAPTER 18: ITINERARY FOR EVERY TRAVELERS............ 178
- Family-Friendly Itinerary............ 178

5

Couples Itinerary... 180
Solo Traveler Itinerary... 182
Adventure Seekers Itinerary.................................183
Group Travel Itinerary.. 185
7-day itinerary.. 187
   Day 1: Explore Marina Bay and Surroundings.... 187
   Day 2: Sentosa Island...................................... 188
   Day 3: Cultural and Historical Exploration.... 189
   Day 4: Nature and Outdoor Adventure.......... 189
   Day 5: Adventure and Wildlife...................... 190
   Day 6: Shopping and Leisure......................... 191
   Day 7: Day Trip to Pulau Ubin and Changi Village..192

CHAPTER 19: TOUR GUIDES AND OPERATORS. 194
   TOURIST TRAPS TO AVOID............................200

CHAPTER 20: ADDITIONAL RESOURCES.......205
   Best Travel Apps for Your Trip............................205

CONCLUSION... 212

SINGAPORE TRAVEL JOURNAL (BONUS)...... 216

INTRODUCTION

Singapore offers a vibrant mix of modern attractions and cultural treasures that appeal to all types of travelers. From its iconic skyline to its hidden gems tucked away in lesser-known neighborhoods, this guide brings you a diverse range of places to visit. Whether you're drawn to bustling city streets or peaceful green spaces, Singapore has something for everyone. This guide provides insights into both famous landmarks and spots that might not be on the usual tourist radar, all presented in a straightforward and easy-to-understand format. No matter your travel experience, this guide will help you uncover the best of what Singapore has to offer.

Singapore is often seen as a small island country, but don't let its size fool you. It is packed with things to do and see. From the moment you arrive, you will notice how modern, clean, and well-organized the city is.

However, beyond the polished exterior lies a rich history and a deep cultural heritage. Singapore is a melting pot of cultures, and this is reflected in everything from its food to its architecture. In this guide, you will learn not only about the famous tourist spots like Marina Bay Sands and Gardens by the Bay but also about the neighborhoods where you can experience the true heart of the city, places that many travelers may overlook.

One of the things that makes Singapore unique is how it blends the old with the new. You can visit ultra-modern shopping malls, and then step into historic temples or traditional markets just a few streets away. The mix of cultures here, including Chinese, Malay, Indian, and Western influences, means that you will never run out of intriguing places to visit or new dishes to try. Singapore's food scene is world-famous, and this guide will also point you to where you can taste the best local dishes.

You will find everything from hawker centers, where you can eat like a local for just a few dollars, to high-end restaurants offering a fine dining experience.

No matter your budget, there's always something delicious to enjoy in Singapore.

Another thing that makes Singapore stand out is how green it is. Despite being a bustling urban center, it is filled with parks, gardens, and nature reserves. This guide takes you to the best green spaces to escape the city and relax. From the famous Botanic Gardens, which is a UNESCO World Heritage site, to hidden parks that most visitors don't know about, you will find plenty of spots to relax and take in the natural beauty. And if you are looking for adventure, there are also outdoor activities like hiking trails that offer stunning views of the city and its surroundings.

For those who love shopping, Singapore is often referred to as a shopper's paradise.

This guide will show you the best places to find great deals, whether you are looking for high-end fashion, electronics, or unique souvenirs to take back home.

Orchard Road is the most famous shopping street, but there are also many hidden shopping areas that locals frequent, offering more affordable options and a different kind of experience. You will find a mix of huge malls, small boutiques, and street markets, each offering something different.

When it comes to culture, Singapore is home to a variety of museums, galleries, and cultural centers that showcase the country's rich history and diversity. This guide will introduce you to the must-visit cultural institutions, such as the National Museum and the Asian Civilizations Museum, where you can learn more about Singapore's past and how it has grown into the modern nation it is today. In addition to the major museums, you will also discover smaller galleries and cultural spaces that are less known but equally fascinating.

These spots often host exhibitions, performances, and events that provide insight into Singapore's creative scene.

Accommodation is another important part of any trip, and Singapore offers a wide range of options to suit all kinds of travelers.

Whether you are looking for luxury hotels, budget-friendly hostels, or something in between, this guide will provide recommendations to help you find the right place to stay. You will also learn about different neighborhoods, so you can choose accommodation that is close to the attractions you want to visit. Each area in Singapore has its character, and staying in the right neighborhood can enhance your overall experience.

Getting around in Singapore is also easy, thanks to its excellent public transportation system. This guide will explain how to use the MRT (Mass Rapid Transit), buses, and taxis to get from one place to another quickly and affordably.

You will also learn about some of the best ways to explore the city on foot, as many of Singapore's top attractions are within walking distance of each other.

The guide also includes tips on how to navigate the city's streets, so you won't waste any time getting lost.

Safety is often a concern for travelers, and Singapore is one of the safest countries in the world. However, this guide will still provide useful safety tips to ensure you have a worry-free trip. From advice on staying safe in busy areas to understanding local laws and customs, you will be well-prepared to enjoy your time in Singapore without any issues. Additionally, you will find information on healthcare facilities and emergency contacts in case you need them during your stay.

Finally, no trip to Singapore would be complete without taking some time to explore the hidden corners of the city that many tourists miss.

This guide is full of recommendations for off-the-beaten-path spots where you can experience a different side of Singapore.

Whether it's a quiet street filled with street art, a rooftop bar with stunning views, or a local market that offers a taste of everyday life, these hidden gems will make your trip even more memorable. You will also discover fun activities that are perfect for families, couples, and solo travelers alike, ensuring that there is something for everyone.

However, this book is packed with valuable information that will help you plan an unforgettable trip to Singapore. It covers everything from well-known attractions to hidden treasures, with tips and advice to suit all types of travelers. Whether you are interested in sightseeing, shopping, dining, or simply soaking up the culture, *Singapore Bucket List* has you covered. So, get ready to explore one of the most exciting destinations in the world, and let this guide be your companion on a journey filled with discovery, excitement, and lasting memories.

WHY YOU OUGHT TO VISIT SINGAPORE

There are many reasons why Singapore should be on your list of must-visit destinations. This small island city-state has earned its reputation as one of the top travel spots in the world, offering a unique mix of modern innovation, rich cultural experiences, and natural beauty. Whether you're an adventure seeker, a food lover, a history buff, or someone who enjoys relaxation, Singapore has something to offer everyone. The moment you arrive, you'll see why it has become a favorite for millions of visitors each year.

First, Singapore's convenient location in Southeast Asia makes it a great starting point for travelers exploring the region. The country's Changi Airport is one of the best and busiest in the world, and flights from here connect to destinations all across Asia and beyond.

This means that if you're planning a multi-country trip, Singapore is a fantastic hub that allows you to easily move from one place to another. The airport itself is an attraction, with plenty of things to do while you're in transit, including shopping, dining, and even visiting an indoor waterfall. Whether you're passing through or staying for a while, Changi Airport ensures that your journey starts smoothly.

Singapore's modern infrastructure is also one of the key reasons why it is a great place to visit. The city is incredibly clean and well-organized, with an efficient public transport system that makes it easy to move around. The MRT (Mass Rapid Transit) system is affordable, fast, and reliable, allowing you to explore the city without any hassle. Taxis and buses are also widely available, and many of the major attractions are within walking distance from one another. As a result, even if you're visiting Singapore for a short time, you can still see and do a lot.

This makes Singapore an ideal destination for those who want to make the most of their trip without having to worry about getting lost or dealing with transportation issues.

One of the main attractions of Singapore is its cultural diversity. Despite its relatively small size, Singapore is home to a variety of cultures, including Chinese, Malay, Indian, and Western influences. This blend of cultures is evident in the city's architecture, food, and festivals. As you walk through different parts of Singapore, you can experience the diversity firsthand. From Chinatown to Little India, each neighborhood has its distinct atmosphere and offers a glimpse into the daily lives and traditions of the people who live there. Visiting these areas allows you to explore different cultures all in one trip without having to leave the city.

Food lovers will find Singapore to be a true paradise. The city is famous for its food scene, which combines flavors from all over the world.

Singaporean cuisine is a reflection of the country's multicultural makeup, with Chinese, Malay, Indian, and Western influences blending in dishes that are both delicious and affordable. Hawker centers, which are open-air food courts, are the best places to try local dishes such as Hainanese chicken rice, laksa, satay, and chili crab. These centers are spread across the city, and they offer a wide variety of dishes at reasonable prices, making them a great option for budget-conscious travelers. At the same time, Singapore is also home to world-class restaurants, so if you're in the mood for fine dining, there are plenty of options to choose from.

Aside from its food, Singapore is also known for its shopping opportunities. Whether you're looking for luxury brands, unique souvenirs, or bargains, Singapore has it all. Orchard Road is one of the most famous shopping streets in the world, lined with high-end malls and designer stores.

However, if you're looking for something a little different, there are plenty of other shopping areas to explore, such as Bugis Street, which is known for its affordable fashion and quirky items, and Haji Lane, which is home to independent boutiques selling handmade goods. Whether you're looking to splurge or just pick up a few gifts for family and friends, Singapore's shopping scene has something for everyone.

Singapore is not just a modern metropolis—it's also one of the greenest cities in the world. Despite being a highly urbanized country, Singapore has made a strong effort to preserve its natural spaces, and as a result, there are plenty of parks and gardens to explore. Gardens by the Bay is one of the city's most iconic attractions, featuring futuristic structures like the Supertree Grove and the Cloud Forest. The Singapore Botanic Gardens, a UNESCO World Heritage site, is another must-visit for nature lovers, offering a peaceful retreat from the busy city streets.

If you enjoy outdoor activities, Singapore also has several nature reserves where you can hike, bird-watch, or simply relax in a natural setting.

The city's commitment to sustainability and green living makes it a great place for eco-conscious travelers who want to enjoy nature while still being in the heart of a bustling city.

History and culture enthusiasts will find plenty to keep them busy in Singapore as well. The city is home to a variety of museums and cultural institutions that tell the story of Singapore's past and present. The National Museum of Singapore is the oldest in the country and offers a comprehensive overview of the city's history, from its early days as a British colony to its rise as a global financial hub. The Asian Civilizations Museum is another highlight, showcasing the rich cultural heritage of Asia and Singapore's role as a crossroads between East and West.

In addition to these major institutions, some smaller museums and galleries focus on specific aspects of Singapore's history and culture, from its diverse ethnic communities to its modern art scene.

Safety is another key reason why you should consider visiting Singapore. The city is one of the safest in the world, with low crime rates and a strong emphasis on law and order. Travelers can explore the city with peace of mind, knowing that they are in a secure environment. This is particularly important for solo travelers and families with children, who can enjoy their trip without worrying about safety concerns. Additionally, Singapore's healthcare system is top-notch, so in the unlikely event that you need medical assistance, you can be confident that you will receive high-quality care.

Another reason why Singapore is a great travel destination is its year-round tropical climate.

There's no need to worry about packing for different seasons, as Singapore's weather is consistently warm and humid. While there are occasional rain showers, they are usually short and won't disrupt your plans. This makes Singapore an ideal destination for travelers who prefer warm weather and want to avoid the cold or harsh winters.

Lastly, Singapore's position as a global financial and business hub means that it is well-equipped to handle the needs of international visitors. English is widely spoken, so language barriers are minimal, and the city's hospitality industry is well-developed, offering a range of services to cater to travelers from all over the world. Whether you're visiting for leisure, business, or a mix of both, Singapore offers the convenience and infrastructure that make travel smooth and enjoyable.

However, Singapore is a destination that has something for everyone. Its blend of cultures, modern attractions, rich history, delicious food, and commitment to sustainability make it a city that can be enjoyed by all types of travelers. Whether you're interested in sightseeing, shopping, dining, or simply relaxing in a beautiful natural setting, Singapore is a destination that will leave a lasting impression. With its welcoming atmosphere, world-class amenities, and endless things to see and do, there's no doubt that a trip to Singapore is an experience worth having.

10 TIPS ON HOW TO USE THIS GUIDE

Here are ten practical tips to help you make the best use of this guide to Singapore's attractions and hidden gems. Following these steps will allow you to plan your trip with confidence and ensure that each day is filled with meaningful and memorable experiences.

1. Start with Your Goals in Mind
Begin by identifying what you hope to experience in Singapore. Whether it's iconic landmarks, local food, cultural experiences, or natural sights, understanding your priorities will help you navigate the guide efficiently.

2. Explore the "Must-See Attractions" Section for Highlights
For a look at Singapore's top sites, visit the Must-See Attractions section.

This part of the guide showcases well-known places like Gardens by the Bay and Marina Bay Sands, detailing why they're worth visiting and providing practical tips like timings and entry fees.

3. Check the "Hidden Gems" for Unique Experiences

The Hidden Gems section is ideal for those looking to discover Singapore's lesser-known spots. Places like Kampong Glam and Pulau Ubin offer unique perspectives of the city and are perfect for travelers wanting an authentic experience. This section includes information on what makes these places special and how to get there.

4. Use the Itineraries to Plan Each Day

To save time and ensure you're seeing a variety of attractions, follow the suggested itineraries provided. These itineraries cater to different types of travelers, from families to solo adventurers, giving you a day-by-day guide for maximizing your visit. Feel free to mix and match to customize your experience.

5. Read the Dining Recommendations for a Culinary Guide

Singapore is famous for its food, so explore the dining section for tips on where to eat based on your budget and taste preferences. This guide includes both affordable hawker centers and higher-end restaurants, offering a wide range of options for every traveler. Each listing also suggests must-try dishes to give you a full taste of Singapore's cuisine.

6. Use the Practical Tips for Smooth Travel

The Helpful Resources section covers essential travel tips, from packing advice to currency information and emergency contacts. This part of the guide is especially useful for first-time visitors as it provides practical advice that will help you prepare for your trip and navigate Singapore confidently.

7. Check Out the Best Photo Spots for Lasting Memories

Singapore has countless photo-worthy spots, and this guide highlights the best places for photography. From scenic views to cultural landmarks, these recommendations offer tips on when and where to capture great shots, helping you document your journey beautifully.

8. Avoid Tourist Traps with Local Insight

To save time and money, the Tourist Traps section shares advice on common pitfalls to avoid, such as overpriced souvenirs and crowded spots. Following these tips will help you have a more genuine and budget-friendly experience.

9. Use the Map and Directions for Easy Navigation

As you plan your day, make use of the map and travel instructions provided for each location. Knowing the MRT stations or best routes to each attraction can help you navigate the city with ease and reduce the time spent on finding directions.

10. Keep the Guide Handy for Quick Reference

Finally, keep this guide accessible throughout your trip, whether in digital or printed form. It's a valuable resource that you can quickly refer to as you move from place to place, ensuring that you always have useful tips and insights at your fingertips.

By following these steps, you'll be able to navigate this guide efficiently, making your trip to Singapore organized, enjoyable, and filled with memorable experiences. Each section of the guide has been thoughtfully crafted to provide valuable information, so use these tips to make the most of your travel adventure.

CHAPTER 1

HISTORY

Singapore's history is both fascinating and complex, shaped by centuries of trade, colonialism, and its strategic location. What started as a small fishing village has grown into one of the most important global financial hubs and one of the world's most visited destinations. Understanding Singapore's history is key to appreciating how it developed into the modern, multicultural city it is today.

Singapore's early history dates back to the 14th century, when it was known as Temasek, meaning "Sea Town." It was a part of the maritime trading network and attracted traders from different parts of the world, including China, India, and the Malay Archipelago. At this time, Singapore was a small but strategic settlement located at the crossroads of major trade routes between Asia and the Middle East.

Its position made it a natural meeting point for traders looking to exchange goods such as spices, silk, and other valuable commodities.

However, Singapore's early significance faded over time as political changes and conflicts in the region shifted power to other kingdoms.

In 1819, modern Singapore was founded by Sir Stamford Raffles, who played a key role in establishing it as a British trading post. This marked a turning point in Singapore's history. At the time, the British were looking for a strategic location in Southeast Asia to secure their interests and strengthen their trade routes. Raffles saw the potential in Singapore's deep natural harbor and its location at the tip of the Malay Peninsula, which made it an ideal place for ships to stop and resupply during long voyages. He negotiated a treaty with the local Malay rulers, allowing the British East India Company to establish a port in Singapore. This move set the foundation for the island's transformation into a major trading hub.

Under British rule, Singapore grew rapidly as merchants from all over the world flocked to the port to trade.

It became a free port, which meant that traders could come and go without having to pay heavy taxes, making it an attractive destination for businesses. This policy of free trade led to a huge increase in shipping activity and brought in immigrants from China, India, Malaysia, and beyond. These early immigrants played a crucial role in building Singapore's economy and contributing to its cultural diversity. As a result, Singapore became a melting pot of different cultures and ethnicities, a characteristic that remains one of the city's most unique and defining features to this day.

Singapore's strategic importance continued to grow throughout the 19th and early 20th centuries, especially during periods of conflict. During World War II, Singapore became a key battleground due to its location.

In 1942, Singapore fell to the Japanese forces, marking the beginning of a challenging period for the island. The occupation lasted until 1945 when Japan surrendered at the end of the war.

The memory of this occupation left a deep impact on Singapore's people, shaping their sense of identity and resilience. Today, places like the Changi Museum and Fort Siloso stand as reminders of this period in Singapore's history, offering insights into the hardships faced by Singaporeans during the war.

After the war, Singapore returned to British control, but the desire for independence grew stronger. The people of Singapore began to push for greater self-governance, and by 1959, Singapore had achieved internal self-rule with its own elected government. However, the road to full independence was not smooth. In 1963, Singapore briefly joined Malaysia, but tensions between the two nations led to Singapore's expulsion just two years later, in 1965.

On August 9, 1965, Singapore became an independent nation, marking the beginning of a new chapter in its history.

At the time of independence, Singapore faced many challenges.

It was a small country with few natural resources, a rapidly growing population, and a lack of housing and jobs. Many people doubted whether the new nation could survive on its own. However, under the leadership of its first Prime Minister, Lee Kuan Yew, Singapore embarked on a remarkable journey of development and modernization. Lee Kuan Yew's vision for Singapore was to turn it into a prosperous and globally competitive city-state. His government focused on education, housing, healthcare, and economic development, laying the groundwork for Singapore's future success.

One of the most significant steps taken during this period was the development of public housing.

The Housing Development Board (HDB) was established in the 1960s to address the severe housing shortage in Singapore. The government launched large-scale public housing projects, providing affordable, modern homes to the growing population.

Today, over 80% of Singaporeans live in HDB flats, and the success of the housing program is considered one of the country's greatest achievements.

In addition to housing, the government also invested heavily in education and infrastructure. Singapore's education system was reformed to focus on skills that would support economic growth, such as science, technology, and engineering. This helped create a highly educated and skilled workforce, which attracted foreign investment and boosted the country's economy.

Meanwhile, massive infrastructure projects, including the construction of the port, airport, and public transportation system, transformed Singapore into a modern and highly efficient city.

Singapore's economy grew rapidly in the decades following independence. The country moved from relying on manufacturing and trade to becoming a global financial hub.

Today, Singapore is known for its advanced economy, which includes industries such as finance, technology, pharmaceuticals, and tourism. It is home to one of the world's busiest ports and is a key player in global trade. Its strategic location and business-friendly environment have attracted multinational companies from around the world, further cementing its status as a global city.

While Singapore's economic success is well known, it is also important to recognize the role of its diverse culture and strong social policies in shaping its identity.

Singapore is a multicultural society, with Chinese, Malay, Indian, and other ethnic groups living together harmoniously. This diversity is celebrated in various festivals, foods, and traditions, making Singapore a vibrant place to visit. The government has also implemented policies to promote racial harmony, ensuring that people of different backgrounds live and work together peacefully.

In recent years, Singapore has continued to evolve. The city has embraced innovation and sustainability, with new developments focusing on creating a greener and more liveable environment. Gardens by the Bay, Marina Barrage, and the Green Plan 2030 are just a few examples of how Singapore is addressing environmental concerns while maintaining its growth. The city's dedication to sustainability is also reflected in its public transportation system, its urban planning, and its emphasis on clean energy and green spaces.

Today, Singapore stands as one of the most prosperous and stable nations in the world.

Its history of resilience, hard work, and forward-thinking policies has transformed it from a small trading post into a thriving global metropolis. Visitors to Singapore can experience the blend of old and new, with historic neighborhoods like Chinatown and Little India sitting alongside ultra-modern developments like Marina Bay Sands and the Central Business District.

Each part of Singapore tells a different story, reflecting the city's journey through time.

However, Singapore's history is one of transformation, innovation, and perseverance. From its early days as a fishing village to its rise as a modern, multicultural city, Singapore's past is woven into every corner of its landscape. As you explore the city, you will find traces of its colonial past, its struggles during World War II, and its remarkable growth in the years following independence.

CHAPTER 2

BEST TIME TO VISIT

When planning a trip to Singapore, one of the first questions many people ask is, "What is the best time to visit?" Singapore's location near the equator means that it has a tropical climate, which stays fairly consistent throughout the year. The weather is generally hot and humid, with temperatures ranging between 25°C and 31°C (77°F to 88°F) all year round. There is no distinct summer or winter in Singapore, so you won't need to worry about packing for different seasons. However, there are some factors to consider that can help you choose the best time for your visit depending on what kind of experience you're looking for.

Singapore experiences two main monsoon seasons, which can impact the amount of rainfall you encounter during your trip.

The first is the Northeast Monsoon, which runs from December to March, and the second is the Southwest Monsoon, from June to September. The Northeast Monsoon is generally the wetter of the two, with more frequent and intense rainfall. During this time, you can expect short, heavy rain showers that may last anywhere from a few minutes to a few hours, but they typically do not last all day. While the rain might briefly disrupt your plans, the good news is that it often clears up quickly, and many indoor attractions, such as museums, shopping malls, and restaurants, can help you pass the time until the weather improves.

The Southwest Monsoon, on the other hand, tends to bring lighter, more scattered rain showers. These showers are less likely to impact your travel plans, as they are typically less intense than those during the Northeast Monsoon. If you are planning to spend a lot of time outdoors, the Southwest Monsoon period may be a slightly more comfortable time to visit in terms of managing rain.

However, as with the Northeast Monsoon, rain showers in Singapore are often short-lived, so they are unlikely to ruin your day.

In between the two monsoon seasons, Singapore experiences periods of relatively drier weather, particularly from March to early June and from September to November. These periods are often considered some of the best times to visit, as you can enjoy warm, sunny days with fewer interruptions from rain. If you're someone who prefers clearer skies for sightseeing, these months may offer the best opportunity to explore outdoor attractions like Gardens by the Bay, Sentosa Island, or the Singapore Zoo without worrying about getting caught in a downpour.

That said, it's important to remember that Singapore's tropical climate means there's always a chance of rain, regardless of when you visit. The high humidity levels, which typically hover around 70–80%, can also make the heat feel more intense, especially for those not used to such conditions.

Wearing lightweight, breathable clothing and staying hydrated are key to staying comfortable while exploring the city.

Apart from the weather, another important factor to consider when deciding the best time to visit Singapore is the city's calendar of events and festivals. Singapore is known for its vibrant cultural diversity, and this is reflected in the many festivals and celebrations that take place throughout the year. Timing your visit to coincide with one of these events can add a unique and memorable dimension to your trip.

For example, if you visit Singapore in January or February, you might be able to experience the Chinese New Year celebrations. This is one of the biggest and most important events in Singapore's calendar, with festivities that last for several days. Streets and buildings are beautifully decorated with red lanterns and lights, and there are parades, fireworks, and cultural performances to enjoy.

Chinatown, in particular, comes alive with special markets, food stalls, and traditional Lion dances. This is a great time to experience the local culture, but it's also one of the busiest periods for travel, so be prepared for larger crowds and higher accommodation prices during this festive season.

In August, Singapore celebrates its National Day, marking the country's independence. National Day is celebrated on August 9th with a grand parade, fireworks displays, and other patriotic events. The festivities often extend for several days, and visitors can enjoy special performances, exhibitions, and other activities around the city. The National Day Parade, in particular, is a highlight, featuring military displays, cultural performances, and a stunning fireworks show over Marina Bay. If you're in Singapore during this time, it's a wonderful opportunity to witness the city's national pride and festive atmosphere.

Another popular time to visit is during the Singapore Grand Prix, usually held in September.

The Grand Prix is part of the Formula 1 World Championship, and Singapore's race is famous for being a night race, where cars speed through the city streets under the lights. Even if you're not a huge motorsport fan, the event brings a lot of excitement to the city, with concerts, parties, and entertainment happening around the race. It's a great time to experience the city's lively nightlife, as well as enjoy the spectacle of the race itself.

In November, Singapore hosts Deepavali (also known as Diwali), which is celebrated by the Indian community. The streets of Little India are illuminated with colorful lights and decorations, and there are various cultural performances, food stalls, and temple events that showcase the richness of Indian traditions. Visiting Singapore during Deepavali gives you the chance to experience a different cultural side of the city, with a focus on light, color, and festivity.

Christmas is also a magical time to visit Singapore, especially for those who enjoy festive lights and decorations. From late November through December, Orchard Road, the city's main shopping district, is transformed into a winter wonderland with elaborate Christmas light displays, decorated trees, and themed installations. Many of the malls and hotels also put up festive decorations, and there are Christmas markets and events around the city. Even though Singapore doesn't experience cold winters, the festive spirit is still very much alive, making it a delightful time to explore the city and enjoy some holiday shopping.

For visitors looking to avoid large crowds and higher prices, it's a good idea to plan your trip outside of the major holiday seasons and peak travel periods. The months of July and October are generally quieter in terms of tourist numbers, and you may find better deals on flights and accommodation during these times.

While the weather remains warm and humid throughout the year, traveling during these off-peak periods can give you more breathing room to enjoy the city's attractions without having to contend with long lines or busy public spaces.

In terms of cost, Singapore is known to be a relatively expensive destination, especially when it comes to accommodation and dining. However, prices for flights, hotels, and attractions can vary depending on the time of year. During peak seasons, such as Chinese New Year, National Day, or the Formula 1 Grand Prix, prices can rise significantly due to increased demand. If you're traveling on a budget, it's worth considering visiting during the shoulder seasons, when prices tend to be more reasonable and you may find better deals on flights and hotels.

Overall, there is no single "best" time to visit Singapore, as the right time depends on your preferences and what you want to experience during your trip.

If you want to avoid rain as much as possible, consider visiting during the drier months between March and June or between September and November.

If you're interested in cultural festivals and events, plan your trip around major celebrations like Chinese New Year, National Day, or the Singapore Grand Prix. No matter when you visit, you're sure to find plenty to see and do in this vibrant, diverse city.

Singapore's weather and festivals offer something for everyone year-round, so it's a destination that can be enjoyed at any time. Whether you prefer exploring outdoor attractions in sunny weather, immersing yourself in the city's cultural festivals, or simply enjoying the food and shopping, Singapore is a destination that has much to offer visitors, no matter when they choose to go.

PACKING THE RIGHT TRAVEL ESSENTIALS

Packing for a trip to Singapore requires some thought, especially if you want to be well-prepared for the city's tropical climate and diverse range of activities.

Since Singapore is located near the equator, the weather is consistently warm and humid throughout the year, with frequent rain showers. The key to packing is to focus on lightweight, breathable clothing and essential items that will keep you comfortable in both the heat and rain, as well as practical accessories for navigating the city.

First, when it comes to clothing, opt for light, breathable fabrics like cotton, linen, or moisture-wicking materials. These fabrics allow your skin to breathe and help you stay cool in Singapore's high humidity. Short-sleeved shirts, T-shirts, and comfortable shorts or lightweight trousers are ideal for daytime exploring.

If you plan on visiting religious or cultural sites, it's a good idea to pack at least one outfit that covers your shoulders and knees, as some places may have dress codes requiring modest attire. For women, a long skirt or lightweight pants paired with a breathable top works well, while men might consider a pair of longer shorts or lightweight trousers with a collared shirt for more formal settings.

Since the weather can change quickly in Singapore, with short bursts of rain even on sunny days, packing a small, portable umbrella or a lightweight rain jacket is essential. These items will come in handy for the sudden showers that are common throughout the year. Singapore's rain usually doesn't last long, but it can be heavy, so having a quick way to stay dry while you're out and about is very useful. If you prefer a rain jacket, make sure it's compact and easy to carry in your bag, as you may only need it for short periods.

Footwear is another important consideration. Since Singapore is a city where walking is the best way to explore many attractions, pack comfortable shoes that are good for walking. Sneakers, walking sandals, or lightweight slip-on shoes with good support are all great options for sightseeing. If you plan to visit more formal venues like fine dining restaurants or attend an event, you may want to pack a nicer pair of shoes, but overall, casual and comfortable footwear will serve you well in most situations.

Also, Singapore's streets and sidewalks are very well maintained, so you won't need hiking boots or heavy-duty shoes unless you're planning to visit nature reserves or hiking trails like the ones at Bukit Timah or MacRitchie Reservoir.

Given Singapore's high levels of humidity, it's also helpful to pack a hat, sunglasses, and sunscreen. A wide-brimmed hat or a baseball cap will protect from the sun while you're walking outdoors.

Sunglasses are a must to protect your eyes from the strong tropical sun, and a high-SPF sunscreen is essential for protecting your skin, especially if you'll be spending time at outdoor attractions like Gardens by the Bay, Sentosa Island, or the Singapore Zoo. Be sure to apply sunscreen regularly, as it can wear off quickly in the heat.

For those planning to visit Singapore's pools, beaches, or water parks like Adventure Cove or Wild Wild Wet, packing swimwear is a must.

You might also want to bring a quick-drying towel or a sarong, which can be useful not just for drying off but also as a cover-up when transitioning between water activities and other parts of your day. Singapore's Sentosa Island has beautiful beaches, so if you enjoy swimming or sunbathing, it's worth having appropriate beachwear packed.

In terms of accessories, carrying a small backpack or crossbody bag can be very practical while exploring Singapore.

It will allow you to store your essentials, such as a water bottle, rain gear, sunscreen, and any purchases you make along the way. A reusable water bottle is especially important in Singapore's heat, as staying hydrated is crucial. While bottled water is widely available for purchase, carrying your water bottle that you can refill saves money and reduces plastic waste. Tap water in Singapore is safe to drink, so you can easily refill your bottle throughout the day.

Technology plays a big role in modern travel, and Singapore is no exception.

If you plan to use your smartphone for navigation, translation, or staying connected, make sure to bring a portable charger or power bank. The heat can drain your phone battery faster than usual, and having a power bank on hand will ensure that your phone stays charged while you're out exploring the city.

Singapore has free Wi-Fi in many public areas, but if you need reliable internet access at all times, consider renting a portable Wi-Fi device or purchasing a local SIM card, both of which are widely available at Changi Airport or around the city.

When it comes to documentation, be sure to pack your passport with at least six months' validity from your date of entry, as this is a requirement for entering Singapore. Additionally, if you need a visa, bring your printed visa confirmation, as well as a copy of your return flight ticket and any hotel bookings. It's a good idea to keep photocopies or digital copies of these documents in case of emergencies.

For convenience, you might also want to download the SG Arrival Card app before traveling, as this will allow you to submit your arrival information electronically, speeding up the process at immigration.

Singapore has a great shopping scene, so while it's always tempting to pack a lot, it's a good idea to leave some space in your suitcase for any purchases you may want to bring back. From luxury goods to local souvenirs, there's plenty to buy in Singapore, whether at Orchard Road's high-end malls or the colorful markets in Chinatown and Little India.

Lastly, a few personal items can make your trip more comfortable. Singapore's efficient public transportation system, including buses and the MRT, is highly air-conditioned, so some people find that carrying a light scarf or shawl helps if they get cold easily while traveling indoors. You might also want to bring some basic medications, such as pain relievers, antihistamines, or any prescription medicines you require.

Pharmacy is widely available in Singapore, but it's always easier to have these essentials with you to avoid searching for them when you need them.

Tips You Need to Know About Visa Requirements

Understanding the visa requirements and entry regulations for Singapore is crucial to ensuring a smooth arrival without complications. While the process is generally simple, the specific requirements can vary depending on your nationality and the length of your stay. First, let's look at the countries that have visa-free access to Singapore. If you hold a passport from certain countries, you may be able to enter Singapore without the need for a visa. This visa-free entry applies mostly to travelers from many Western and Southeast Asian countries, as well as a few others around the world. Citizens of countries such as the United States, the United Kingdom, Australia, Canada, New Zealand, and most European Union countries can enter Singapore without a visa for stays of up to 30 or 90 days, depending on the specific agreements Singapore has with each country.

For example, travelers from the U.S., Canada, and most EU countries are permitted to stay for up to 90 days, while those from Australia and the United Kingdom can stay for 30 days. Citizens of ASEAN (Association of Southeast Asian Nations) member countries like Malaysia, Indonesia, Thailand, and the Philippines also enjoy visa-free access, usually for 30 days.

If your country is not on the visa-exempt list, or if you plan to stay for longer than the permitted period, you will need to apply for a tourist visa before traveling to Singapore. The application process for a Singapore tourist visa is relatively simple and can usually be done online. The first step is to check the official Immigration and Checkpoints Authority (ICA) website to confirm whether you need a visa and what specific documents are required for your application.

In general, you will need to submit a completed visa application form, a passport-sized photograph, a copy of your passport (which should be valid for at least six months from your planned date of entry), and proof of onward travel, such as a return flight ticket. Additionally, you may need to provide details of your accommodation in Singapore and evidence of sufficient funds to support your stay, such as bank statements.

In many cases, you can apply for a Singapore tourist visa online through Singapore's official e-visa system or an authorized visa agent in your home country. Processing times for visa applications are generally fast, taking between three and five working days. However, it's advisable to apply for your visa at least two weeks before your planned travel date to allow for any unforeseen delays. Once your visa is approved, you will receive an electronic visa, which you should print and carry with you when traveling.

For long-term visitors, such as those planning to stay in Singapore for more than 90 days, there are additional visa options available. If you are traveling for business, study, or employment, you will need to apply for the appropriate visa or pass, such as the Employment Pass, S Pass, or Student Pass, depending on the purpose of your visit. The application process for these long-term visas is more detailed, and you may need to provide additional documents such as an employment contract, a letter of acceptance from a school or university, or other supporting materials. It's important to ensure that you have the correct visa for your situation, as overstaying or violating visa conditions can result in fines, deportation, or a ban from entering Singapore in the future.

Once you have your visa (if needed), the next step is understanding Singapore's immigration procedures and entry points. Singapore has several entry points, with the most common being Changi Airport, which is one of the busiest and most efficient airports in the world.

If you are arriving by air, immigration procedures at Changi Airport are straightforward. Upon arrival, you will proceed to the immigration counters, where an officer will check your passport, visa (if required), and arrival card. An arrival card is a simple form that asks for details such as your name, nationality, flight number, and the address where you will be staying in Singapore. You can fill this out on the plane before landing or complete the process electronically using the ICA's SG Arrival Card e-service before your trip.

For travelers entering Singapore by land, there are two main entry points from Malaysia: the Woodlands Checkpoint (connecting to Johor Bahru) and the Tuas Checkpoint. The immigration procedures at these checkpoints are similar to those at the airport. You will need to present your passport and visa (if applicable) and fill out an arrival card.

For those arriving by sea, Singapore also has ferry terminals, such as the Harbourfront Centre and Tanah Merah Ferry Terminal, which handle passengers arriving from nearby islands in Indonesia and Malaysia.

Now, let's talk about the documents you will need for entry into Singapore. Regardless of whether you require a visa or not, there are several key documents that all travelers must have when arriving in Singapore. First, you need a valid passport with at least six months' validity from the date you intend to enter the country. This is a common requirement for most international travel and ensures that your passport remains valid for the duration of your stay. You will also need a completed arrival card (either paper or electronic), which provides basic information about your visit.

In addition to your passport and arrival card, immigration officers may ask to see proof of onward travel, such as a return or onward flight ticket, to confirm that you do not intend to overstay in Singapore. It is also a good idea to have a copy of your accommodation booking and proof of sufficient funds to support your stay, although these documents are not always requested. If you are visiting for business, study, or other long-term purposes, be sure to have your visa or relevant pass on hand as well.

Finally, it's important to be aware of Singapore's customs regulations before you travel. Singapore has strict rules about what can be brought into the country, and travelers should be prepared to declare certain items upon arrival. For example, the import of chewing gum is prohibited, except for therapeutic gum prescribed by a doctor. There are also strict regulations on the importation of tobacco products, alcohol, and electronic cigarettes. Travelers are allowed to bring limited quantities of duty-free alcohol, but any excess must be declared and subject to customs duties.

Certain items, such as drugs, firearms, and explosives, are strictly prohibited and can result in severe penalties, including imprisonment or even the death penalty. Singapore also has strict laws on bringing in pirated goods, counterfeit products, or obscene materials. It's important to familiarize yourself with these regulations before traveling to avoid any issues at customs.

Additionally, if you are carrying more than SGD 20,000 (or the equivalent in other currencies) in cash, you are required to declare this to customs upon arrival. This rule is in place to prevent money laundering and other illegal activities, so make sure you are aware of the limits if you plan to bring large amounts of cash into the country.

Moreover, whether you are visiting Singapore for a short holiday or planning a longer stay, it's crucial to be well-informed about the visa requirements and entry procedures to ensure a smooth trip.

From understanding whether your country allows for visa-free access to preparing the necessary documents for entry and complying with customs regulations, taking the time to plan ahead will make your arrival in Singapore stress-free. Keep in mind the specific rules and regulations related to visas, immigration, and customs, and you will be well-prepared to enjoy everything that this exciting city-state has to offer.

However, packing for your trip to Singapore is all about being prepared for warm, humid weather, with some light rain mixed in. Lightweight, breathable clothing, comfortable shoes, and sun protection are your top priorities, along with a few practical items like a small umbrella and a reusable water bottle. Packing these essentials will help you stay comfortable and make the most of your time exploring this exciting and diverse city.

PHRASES TOURIST SHOULD KNOW FOR EASY COMMUNICATION

When visiting Singapore, knowing a few helpful phrases can make interactions with locals smoother and more enjoyable. Singaporeans speak English as one of the official languages, but you may also hear Singlish, a unique local dialect that blends English with Malay, Chinese, Tamil, and other regional languages. Here are some essential phrases and expressions that can be very useful for tourists:

1. "Can?" – This short phrase is commonly used to ask if something is possible or allowed, similar to saying "Is that okay?" or "Can I?" For example, "Can I sit here? Can?"

2. "Lah" – You might hear locals adding "lah" at the end of sentences for emphasis. It's a very common part of Singlish. For example, "It's really nice, lah!" or "No need, lah."

3. **"Shiok"** – This expression is used to describe something that feels or tastes really good, especially food. For example, "This laksa is shiok!" meaning it tastes amazing.

4. **"Kopi" and "Teh"** – If you're ordering coffee or tea, these words are commonly used in hawker centers. "Kopi" means coffee, and "Teh" means tea. There are also variations like "kopi-o" (black coffee) and "teh tarik" (pulled tea with milk).

5. **"How much?"** – Asking about prices is simple with "How much?" but in Singlish, you might hear it as "How much ah?" which is a friendlier way to check the price of something at a market or stall.

6. **"Paiseh"** – This means to feel shy, embarrassed, or apologetic. Locals might use it when they feel they are inconveniencing someone. For example, "Paiseh, can I get by?" when asking someone to move aside.

7. "Auntie" and "Uncle" – In Singapore, it's common to address older people as "Auntie" or "Uncle," which is a respectful way to speak to them, especially in markets or hawker centers. "Auntie, how much for this?"

8. "Tapao" – This means to take food to go or for takeaway. If you want to take your meal with you, you can say "I'd like to tapao, please."

9. "Chop" – This word is used to reserve a place or mark something. For example, if you place a packet of tissues on a table at a hawker center, it's a sign that the table is reserved, or "chopped."

10. "Where is…?" – Locals are very helpful when it comes to giving directions. To ask for directions, you can start by saying "Where is" followed by the place name, such as "Where is MRT?" or "Where is Merlion Park?"

11. "Excuse me" – It's good to know that "excuse me" is widely understood, but you can also say, "Can I trouble you?" which is a polite way to ask for help.

12. "Lobang" – This term means a good deal or tip-off. If someone gives you a "lobang," they're giving you useful information, like a recommendation for an affordable place to eat or shop.

13. "Siao" – This means "crazy" or "mad." It's used humorously among friends when something seems unbelievable. For example, "$20 for this small drink? Siao!"

14. "So how?" – This phrase is used to ask for someone's opinion or to decide what to do next. For example, "We missed the last bus. So how?"

15. "Makan" – Meaning "eat" in Malay, is commonly used by locals when talking about food. For example, "Let's go makan" means "Let's go eat."

These phrases can help you blend in with locals, make it easier to navigate public spaces, and give you a taste of Singapore's unique language culture. Knowing these expressions will not only help you communicate effectively but also give you a more authentic connection to the local culture.

CHAPTER 3

HOW TO ARRIVE

Getting to Singapore is straightforward and convenient thanks to the country's position as a major global travel hub. Whether you're flying from a neighboring country in Southeast Asia or from across the globe, Singapore's Changi Airport connects the city to almost every part of the world. Once you arrive, getting from the airport to the city center is easy, with multiple transport options available. Additionally, once you're in the city, Singapore's public transport system is efficient, clean, and easy to navigate. Whether you prefer to use buses, the MRT (Mass Rapid Transit), taxis, or ride-hailing apps, Singapore offers plenty of options for getting around. For those who prefer more flexibility, renting a car is also an option, though it might not always be necessary given how well-connected the city is.

Here's an in-depth look at how to get to Singapore and navigate the city once you're there.

First, let's talk about the best airlines flying to Singapore. Singapore's Changi Airport is consistently ranked as one of the best airports in the world, and it serves as a hub for many leading international airlines. If you're flying from major cities in Asia, Europe, North America, or Australia, you'll have plenty of options to choose from. Singapore Airlines, the country's national carrier, is known for its excellent service and frequent flights to many global destinations. It's often the top choice for travelers flying to Singapore, offering a comfortable and reliable travel experience. Other popular airlines flying to Singapore include Emirates, Qatar Airways, and Cathay Pacific for those coming from the Middle East or Asia, as well as British Airways, Lufthansa, and Air France for European routes. From North America, airlines such as United Airlines, Delta, and Qantas offer routes to Singapore with both direct and connecting flights.

Budget airlines like Scoot, Jetstar, and AirAsia are also worth considering if you're traveling within Southeast Asia and looking for more affordable fares.

Once you land at Changi Airport, the next step is getting to the city. Changi is located about 20 kilometers from the city center, and there are several convenient transportation options to get you there. The most affordable and popular option is the MRT, Singapore's efficient train system. Changi Airport has its own MRT station, located at Terminals 2 and 3, and you can easily catch a train into the city. The MRT takes about 30-40 minutes to reach central areas such as City Hall or Raffles Place, and trains are frequent, with services starting early in the morning and running until midnight. This makes it a great option for most travelers, especially if you're looking to avoid traffic.

For those who prefer door-to-door service, taxis are readily available at the airport and provide a fast and comfortable way to reach your hotel or accommodation. The taxi ride from Changi to the city center takes around 20 to 30 minutes, depending on traffic, and fares are generally reasonable. Expect to pay between SGD 20 to SGD 40, depending on the time of day (there may be additional charges during peak hours, late at night, or for rides originating from the airport). Taxis in Singapore are metered, so you won't need to worry about negotiating fares. Additionally, taxi drivers in Singapore are known for being polite and professional, and they usually speak English, making it easy to communicate.

If you're looking for a more budget-friendly alternative to taxis, Singapore's ride-hailing apps, such as Grab and Gojek, offer another convenient way to get from Changi Airport to your destination.

These services work similarly to Uber and allow you to book a ride through the app on your smartphone. Grab, in particular, is widely used in Singapore, and it's often cheaper than regular taxis.

You can pay directly through the app using your credit card, which can be a more convenient option if you don't have local currency upon arrival.

Once you're in the city, Singapore's public transport system is one of the best ways to get around. The MRT is the backbone of the system, with an extensive network of lines that connect most of the city's major attractions, shopping districts, and neighborhoods. The trains are clean, air-conditioned, and always on time. The MRT is also very easy to use, with clear signs in English, and the stations are well-marked. To use the MRT, you can purchase single-trip tickets at the station or get an EZ-Link card, which is a rechargeable card that allows you to tap in and out of trains and buses without needing to buy tickets each time.

The EZ-Link card is recommended if you'll be using public transport frequently, as it saves time and offers a small discount on fares.

In addition to the MRT, Singapore's bus system is also highly efficient and covers areas that may not be reachable by train. Buses in Singapore are clean, air-conditioned, and run on time, making them a great option for short trips. Like the MRT, you can use your EZ-Link card to pay for bus rides, and there are clear signs at bus stops to help you figure out which bus to take. Most buses display information in English, and there are even apps that provide real-time updates on bus arrivals, which is handy when planning your trips.

For those who prefer more flexibility in getting around, taxis and ride-hailing apps are always available. Taxis can be hailed from the street, found at taxi stands, or booked via phone or app. They are a comfortable and reliable way to get around the city, especially if you're traveling in a group or have heavy luggage.

Grab, the most popular ride-hailing app in Singapore offers various services ranging from budget-friendly rides to more luxurious options, depending on your preferences and budget.

If you're considering renting a car and driving in Singapore, it's important to be aware that while driving offers flexibility, it's not always the most practical option for most travelers. Singapore has an excellent public transport system, and the city's road network is often busy, especially during peak hours. Traffic congestion and high parking fees in central areas can make driving less appealing compared to using public transport. However, if you prefer the convenience of having your vehicle or if you're planning to explore areas outside the city, such as Sentosa Island or nature reserves, car rentals are available at Changi Airport and various locations throughout the city. International car rental companies such as Hertz, Avis, and Budget operate in Singapore, as well as local companies. To rent a car, you'll need a valid international driving permit or a driving license in English.

Keep in mind that Singapore drives on the left-hand side of the road and strict traffic rules are enforced, including speed limits, parking regulations, and the use of seatbelts.

Overall, getting to Singapore and navigating the city is incredibly easy and convenient. Whether you prefer to use public transport, taxis, or drive yourself, Singapore's well-developed infrastructure ensures that getting around is smooth and stress-free. The choice of transportation depends on your personal preferences, but most travelers find that the MRT and buses offer the best combination of affordability and convenience.

CHAPTER 4

GETTING AROUND

Getting around Singapore is easy, thanks to the city's well-planned transportation system. Whether you want to explore by public transport, bike, or even on foot, there are plenty of convenient options to help you reach every corner of the city. Singapore is known for its efficient, clean, and affordable transport services, making it simple for tourists to get around without needing a car. One of the best ways to get around Singapore is by using its public transport system. The backbone of this system is the MRT (Mass Rapid Transit), which is Singapore's subway network.

The MRT is fast, clean, and well-organized, with stations located near most major attractions, shopping centers, and neighborhoods. It's an ideal choice for tourists because it connects the city center with areas such as Marina Bay, Orchard Road, Chinatown, Little India, and Sentosa Island.

The trains are air-conditioned, which is a relief in Singapore's hot and humid weather, and they run frequently, so you'll rarely need to wait long. Signs and announcements are in English, making it easy to navigate even if you're unfamiliar with the city.

To use the MRT, you can buy a single-trip ticket or, more conveniently, get an EZ-Link card. The EZ-Link card is a rechargeable card that you can tap in and out at the gates, much like a contactless payment card. You can top it up at machines in the station or convenience stores, and it works on both MRT trains and buses, making it the most flexible option for public transport.

The MRT operates from around 5:30 am to midnight, and with several lines, including the North-South, East-West, and Circle lines, you'll find that it covers most of the places you'll want to visit.

In addition to the MRT, Singapore's bus system is another great way to get around.

The buses in Singapore are air-conditioned, reliable, and cover areas that may not be reachable by MRT. Buses are a good choice if you want to take a scenic route and see more of the city above ground, or if you're traveling to places like Singapore Botanic Gardens or the outer neighborhoods. Like the MRT, you can use your EZ-Link card to pay for bus rides, and there are detailed maps and signs at bus stops that provide information about routes. Bus rides are smooth and frequent, making it easy to explore even the quieter parts of Singapore.

For a more active way of getting around, cycling is becoming an increasingly popular option in Singapore.

The city has worked hard to develop cycling infrastructure, and there are now many designated bike lanes and park connectors where you can safely ride a bicycle. One of the best ways to rent a bike is through shared bike services such as SG Bike or Anywheel, which allow you to pick up and drop off bikes at various locations around the city using a mobile app. Cycling is a great way to explore areas like East Coast Park, the Marina Bay waterfront, or the many scenic parks and gardens across the island. Some attractions, like Pulau Ubin, are especially suited for cycling, and it's a fun, eco-friendly way to see the sights.

For tourists who enjoy walking, Singapore has plenty of well-maintained paths and walking routes that are both enjoyable and practical. One of the best walking routes is along Marina Bay, where you can stroll around the bay and take in views of iconic landmarks like the Marina Bay Sands, ArtScience Museum, and the Merlion.

Another popular walking route is the Southern Ridges, a series of elevated walkways and paths that take you through parks and forested areas, offering beautiful views of the city and harbor. The Orchard Road shopping district is also a great area to explore on foot, with wide sidewalks and plenty of attractions, restaurants, and shops along the way.

Walking in Singapore is easy thanks to the city's pedestrian-friendly layout, with many paths shaded by trees or covered walkways that offer protection from the sun and rain.

When it comes to more flexible options, taxis are widely available in Singapore and offer a comfortable way to travel, especially if you're carrying luggage or prefer door-to-door service. Taxis can be hailed from the street, found at designated taxi stands, or booked through apps. All taxis in Singapore are metered, and fares are relatively affordable compared to other major cities. However, there are additional surcharges during peak hours, for airport trips, or late at night.

Taxi drivers in Singapore generally speak English and are professional, so you won't have trouble explaining your destination. For those who prefer ride-sharing services, Grab and Gojek are the two most popular apps in Singapore, offering services similar to Uber.

These apps allow you to book rides quickly and easily through your phone, and you can pay either through the app or in cash.

For tourists looking for the best value and convenience when traveling around Singapore, day passes and transportation tickets are a great option. The Singapore Tourist Pass is a popular choice for visitors who plan to use public transport frequently. This pass allows unlimited travel on the MRT, LRT, and buses for one, two, or three days, depending on which option you choose. It's a cost-effective way to explore the city without worrying about topping up an EZ-Link card. You can purchase the Singapore Tourist Pass at various MRT stations, including Changi Airport, and it's easy to use by simply tapping it at the gates.

Another option is the Standard Ticket, which is a stored-value ticket that can be used for a single journey on the MRT.

These tickets are available at machines in MRT stations, and while they are convenient for one-off trips, they're not as flexible or economical as the EZ-Link card or Singapore Tourist Pass for tourists who will be making multiple trips.

Finally, getting around Singapore is easy, convenient, and affordable thanks to its efficient public transport system, well-maintained roads, and various transport options. Whether you're taking the MRT, hopping on a bus, renting a bike, walking, or using a taxi, the city is designed to make travel simple for both residents and visitors alike. With an EZ-Link card or a Singapore Tourist Pass, you'll have access to all the public transport you need, allowing you to explore everything from iconic attractions to hidden gems across the island. No matter how you choose to travel, Singapore's transport system ensures that you can move around the city with ease and enjoy all that it has to offer.

CHAPTER 5

OPTIONS FOR ACCOMMODATION

Singapore offers a wide range of accommodation options that suit various budgets and preferences, making it an ideal destination for travelers seeking comfort, convenience, and unique experiences. From luxurious resorts and hotels to more affordable options and specialized lodging, Singapore provides high-quality accommodations that allow you to fully enjoy the city's vibrant attractions.

Luxury Resorts and Hotels

For travelers looking to indulge in Singapore's high-end hospitality, the city is home to some of the world's most luxurious resorts and hotels. One of the most iconic luxury accommodations is *Marina Bay Sands*, known for its striking architecture and world-class amenities.

Staying at Marina Bay Sands offers not only luxury but also direct access to the famous SkyPark infinity pool, which provides breathtaking views of the city skyline. The hotel is also connected to a range of high-end shopping, dining, and entertainment options, including the ArtScience Museum and Gardens by the Bay. To reach Marina Bay Sands, you can take the MRT to Bayfront Station (Circle Line or Downtown Line).

Another top luxury hotel is *The Fullerton Hotel Singapore*, housed in a historic building that was once Singapore's General Post Office. The Fullerton Hotel blends timeless elegance with modern comfort, offering spacious rooms, fine dining, and a prime location near the Marina Bay waterfront. The hotel is within walking distance of Merlion Park, the Esplanade, and other key attractions. For those who want to experience a more resort-like atmosphere, *Capella Singapore* on Sentosa Island offers a tranquil retreat surrounded by lush greenery and stunning views of the South China Sea.

The resort combines colonial-style architecture with contemporary luxury, and guests have easy access to Sentosa's beaches, golf courses, and attractions like Universal Studios Singapore.

Affordable Accommodation

If you're looking for more budget-friendly options without compromising comfort, Singapore has a variety of affordable hotels and hostels that provide excellent value for money. One of the most popular choices for budget travelers is *Hotel 81*, which has several branches across the city, including in areas like Chinatown, Geylang, and Bugis. These hotels offer basic amenities at affordable prices, making them a great option for solo travelers, couples, or groups looking to save on accommodation costs. The rooms are clean and comfortable, and the locations are convenient for accessing public transport, such as the MRT, to explore the city.

For travelers seeking a mix of affordability and character, *The Pod Boutique Capsule Hotel* in the Bugis area offers a unique take on budget lodging.

This capsule hotel provides individual sleeping pods that offer privacy while also being wallet-friendly. The Pod is perfect for solo travelers who want a more modern, minimalist setting while enjoying perks like free breakfast and easy access to nearby attractions like Bugis Junction and Haji Lane. You can reach The Pod by taking the MRT to Bugis Station (East-West Line or Downtown Line).

Ibis Budget Singapore is another affordable option with branches across the city, including locations in Balestier, Joo Chiat, and Geylang. These hotels offer simple, comfortable rooms with modern facilities like free Wi-Fi and air conditioning, providing a practical and budget-friendly stay. The locations are close to MRT stations, making it easy to get around the city without spending too much on accommodation.

Specialized Lodging Experiences

For travelers looking for something a little different, Singapore offers specialized lodging experiences that provide a unique twist to the standard hotel stay. One option is staying in *heritage hotels*, which are often converted colonial buildings or shophouses that retain their historic charm while offering modern comforts. An excellent example is *Hotel Fort Canning*, located in the heart of Fort Canning Park. This boutique hotel is set in a former British military base and combines historic architecture with luxurious amenities, offering a peaceful escape within the city's greenery. Guests can enjoy walks in the park or explore nearby attractions like the National Museum of Singapore. To get there, take the MRT to Dhoby Ghaut Station (North-South, North-East, and Circle Lines).

For nature lovers, *Garden Asia Resort* in the Kranji Countryside offers a retreat surrounded by nature. This eco-friendly resort focuses on sustainability and provides farm-style accommodation where guests can relax in a more rural setting, away from the city's busy streets. The resort also organizes farm tours and outdoor activities, making it a great option for travelers interested in eco-tourism and a slower-paced experience.

To reach Garden Asia Resort, take the MRT to Kranji Station (North-South Line), and then a short taxi ride will take you to the resort.

For those who want to stay somewhere a little out of the ordinary, *Hotel Mono* in Chinatown offers an Instagram-worthy experience. This boutique hotel is housed in a row of six restored heritage shophouses and features a minimalist black-and-white design that appeals to modern travelers. The rooms are stylish and contemporary, while the location in the heart of Chinatown means you'll be surrounded by culture, history, and vibrant food markets. Hotel Mono is just a short walk from Chinatown MRT Station (North-East Line and Downtown Line).

In conclusion, Singapore's range of accommodation options ensures that every traveler, whether seeking luxury, affordability, or a unique lodging experience, will find a place that suits their needs.

The city's efficient public transport system, including the MRT and buses, makes it easy to travel between attractions and your chosen accommodation, no matter where you stay. Whether you're lounging by the pool at Marina Bay Sands, enjoying a budget-friendly room at Hotel 81, or exploring history at Hotel Fort Canning, you can be sure that Singapore's accommodations will provide a comfortable base for your adventure.

CHAPTER 6
MUST-SEE ATTRACTIONS

Singapore is filled with must-see attractions that offer something for everyone, from breathtaking gardens to iconic landmarks and world-class museums. These attractions showcase Singapore's unique ability to blend nature, modern architecture, culture, and entertainment into one unforgettable experience.

Gardens By The Bay

Starting with *Gardens by the Bay*, this futuristic garden is one of Singapore's most iconic attractions. Located in the heart of the city, near Marina Bay, Gardens by the Bay covers 101 hectares and features stunningly landscaped gardens, towering supertrees, and two massive conservatories.

The most famous parts of Gardens by the Bay are the Flower Dome and the Cloud Forest, two giant glass domes that house a wide range of plants from all over the world. The Flower Dome is the largest glass greenhouse in the world and showcases a variety of flowers and plants from Mediterranean and semi-arid regions. You'll see olive trees, baobabs, and colorful seasonal flowers. The Cloud Forest is equally impressive, with a tall indoor waterfall and lush greenery that mimics tropical mountain regions.

One of the highlights of the gardens is the *Supertree Grove*, a group of giant tree-like structures covered in vertical gardens. These Supertrees light up at night during the Garden Rhapsody, a free light and sound show that takes place daily. You can also take the OCBC Skyway, a walkway that connects two of the Supertrees, offering stunning views of the gardens and Marina Bay. To get to Gardens by the Bay, you can take the MRT and alight at Bayfront Station on the Circle or Downtown Line.

The garden is just a short walk from the station, and there are clear signs guiding you to the main entrance.

Marina Bay Sand

Next is the *Marina Bay Sands SkyPark*, located atop the Marina Bay Sands Hotel, one of Singapore's most recognizable buildings. The SkyPark is a large observation deck that offers panoramic views of the city skyline, Marina Bay, and beyond. Standing 200 meters above the ground, the SkyPark gives visitors a bird's-eye view of famous landmarks like the Singapore Flyer, Gardens by the Bay, and the nearby skyscrapers. The SkyPark also features the world's largest rooftop infinity pool, though access to the pool is reserved for hotel guests. Even if you're not staying at the hotel, visiting the observation deck is a must for anyone wanting to take in the best views of the city. To get to Marina Bay Sands, take the MRT to Bayfront Station on the Circle or Downtown Line and follow the signs leading to the hotel.

Sentosa Island

Sentosa Island is another must-see destination in Singapore. Known as Singapore's island resort,

Sentosa offers a wide range of attractions, including beaches, nature trails, luxury hotels, and theme parks. One of the island's most popular attractions is *Universal Studios Singapore*, which is part of Resorts World Sentosa. Universal Studios offers exciting rides, shows, and attractions based on popular films and television shows. Whether you're visiting with family or just looking for some fun, the theme park has something for everyone, from thrilling roller coasters like Battlestar Galactica to family-friendly rides like Madagascar: A Crate Adventure. Outside the theme park, Sentosa is also home to beautiful beaches like Siloso Beach and Palawan Beach, where you can relax, swim, or try water sports. To reach Sentosa, take the MRT to Harbourfront Station on the North-East Line or Circle Line, and then either take the Sentosa Express from VivoCity shopping mall or ride the cable car from Mount Faber for scenic views.

Singapore Flyer

The *Singapore Flyer* is another attraction that offers incredible views of the city. Standing at 165 meters tall, this giant Ferris wheel is one of the largest in the world. A ride on the Singapore Flyer takes about 30 minutes and provides 360-degree views of the city, including Marina Bay, the Singapore River, and even parts of Malaysia and Indonesia on a clear day. Each capsule of the Flyer is spacious and air-conditioned, allowing you to relax and take in the sights as you rotate slowly above the city. The Singapore Flyer is located near Marina Bay and is easily accessible via the MRT. Take the Circle Line to Promenade Station, and it's just a short walk to the flyer.

Merlion Park

No visit to Singapore is complete without stopping by *Merlion Park*, home to the famous Merlion statue. The Merlion, which has the head of a lion and the body of a fish, is a national symbol of Singapore.

The statue represents Singapore's origins as a fishing village and its name, which means "Lion City." Merlion Park is located at the waterfront in Marina Bay, offering great views of the Marina Bay Sands Hotel and the surrounding skyline. It's a popular spot for tourists to take photos and enjoy the scenery, especially in the evening when the lights of the nearby buildings reflect off the water. To get to Merlion Park, take the MRT to Raffles Place Station on the North-South or East-West Line, and it's just a short walk to the park.

National Gallery Singapore and The ArtScience Museum

For art and culture lovers, the National *Gallery Singapore* and the *ArtScience Museum* are must-visit attractions. The National Gallery Singapore is home to the largest public collection of modern art in Southeast Asia. The gallery is housed in two beautifully restored historic buildings—the former Supreme Court and City Hall—and showcases over 8,000 works of art from

Singaporean and Southeast Asian artists. Exhibitions at the National Gallery range from traditional paintings and sculptures to contemporary multimedia installations. Visitors can spend hours exploring the different galleries, learning about the region's rich art history, and admiring the stunning architecture of the building itself. The gallery is located in the Civic District, and the nearest MRT station is City Hall Station on the North-South and East-West Lines.

The *ArtScience Museum*, located at Marina Bay Sands, is another great stop for those interested in the intersection of art, science, and technology. The museum is known for its unique lotus-shaped design and features interactive exhibitions that explore topics such as space exploration, nature, and the future of technology. One of the museum's most popular permanent exhibitions is "Future World," which features digital art installations that respond to touch and movement, creating an immersive experience for visitors of all ages.

The ArtScience Museum is just a short walk from Bayfront MRT Station on the Circle and Downtown Lines.

However, Singapore's must-see attractions offer a diverse range of experiences that reflect the city's mix of nature, culture, and modernity. From the futuristic gardens and Supertrees at Gardens by the Bay to the world-class views at Marina Bay Sands SkyPark and the Singapore Flyer, there's no shortage of breathtaking sights. Whether you're exploring Sentosa's beaches and theme parks, taking in the art at the National Gallery, or snapping a photo at Merlion Park, these attractions are sure to make your trip to Singapore memorable. Each attraction is also easily accessible via Singapore's efficient public transportation system, making it convenient to explore all the city has to offer.

CHAPTER 7

HIDDEN GEMS

Singapore is a city known for its famous landmarks and modern attractions, but it also has several hidden gems that offer a glimpse into the city's cultural heritage, natural beauty, and lesser-known treasures. These hidden gems provide a unique experience for travelers looking to go beyond the well-known tourist spots and discover more of Singapore's rich diversity. One of Singapore's quirkiest attractions is *Haw Par Villa*, a theme park that offers a very different kind of cultural experience. Originally built in 1937 by the creators of Tiger Balm, this park is dedicated to Chinese folklore, mythology, and legends.

It is best known for its colorful and sometimes bizarre statues and dioramas that depict various moral stories, including scenes from the afterlife as portrayed in the "Ten Courts of Hell."

The park is both educational and unusual, providing visitors with a deeper understanding of Chinese values and teachings, but in a way that is truly one of a kind. If you're looking for something offbeat and culturally rich, Haw Par Villa is a must-see. To get there, take the MRT to Haw Par Villa Station on the Circle Line, and the park is just a short walk from the station.

For those who want to escape the hustle and bustle of the city, *Pulau Ubin* offers a rustic, nature-filled retreat. Located off the northeastern coast of Singapore, Pulau Ubin is one of the last remaining areas in Singapore that showcases the country's traditional kampong (village) lifestyle. The island is a haven for nature lovers, with its diverse ecosystems of mangroves, forests, and wetlands.

One of the highlights is the Chek Jawa Wetlands, a rich natural habitat that is home to a variety of wildlife, including monitor lizards, crabs, and sea creatures.

Visitors can explore the island by renting a bicycle and cycling along the quiet trails, or simply walk and take in the serene surroundings. To get to Pulau Ubin, you'll need to take a boat from Changi Point Ferry Terminal. The ride takes about 10 minutes, and ferries run regularly throughout the day.

If you're interested in exploring Singapore's natural landscapes without leaving the city, the *Southern Ridges* offer a perfect blend of urban and natural environments. This 10-kilometer network of trails connects several parks and green spaces, providing stunning views of both the city skyline and lush greenery. The highlight of the Southern Ridges is the Henderson Waves Bridge, Singapore's highest pedestrian bridge, which features a unique wave-like structure.

The trails take you through places like Mount Faber Park, HortPark, and Kent Ridge Park, offering a peaceful escape into nature while still being close to the city.

The Southern Ridges are ideal for walking, birdwatching, and photography, making it a great spot for those who want to experience a different side of Singapore. To start your journey, you can take the MRT to Harbourfront Station on the North-East Line or Circle Line and begin the walk from Mount Faber Park.

Kampong Glam is one of Singapore's most culturally rich areas, offering a glimpse into the city's Malay heritage. This historic district is centered around the majestic Sultan Mosque, a key landmark in Singapore. Kampong Glam was traditionally a Malay and Muslim quarter, and today it is a vibrant neighborhood filled with colorful shophouses, boutiques, and cafés. Haji Lane, in particular, is known for its eclectic mix of street art, independent stores, and trendy restaurants.

Visitors can learn more about the history of the area by visiting the Malay Heritage Centre, which showcases the culture and traditions of Singapore's Malay community.

Kampong Glam is also home to many Middle Eastern and Malay eateries, making it a fantastic place to try local dishes like nasi padang or kebabs. To get to Kampong Glam, take the MRT to Bugis Station on the East-West Line or Downtown Line, and the neighborhood is just a short walk away.

For a completely different experience, head to the *Kranji Countryside*, a rural area in the northwestern part of Singapore that is home to several farms and nature reserves. This area offers a refreshing break from the urban landscape, allowing visitors to explore Singapore's agricultural side. You can visit farms such as Hay Dairies, where you can watch goat milking and buy fresh goat milk, or Bollywood Veggies, an organic farm that grows a wide variety of fruits and vegetables. The Kranji Countryside also offers opportunities for farm-to-table dining, with several restaurants serving up fresh produce from local farms. If you enjoy learning about sustainable farming practices or simply want to experience a different, more rural side of Singapore, the Kranji Countryside is a hidden gem worth visiting. To get there, take the MRT to Kranji Station on the North-South Line, and then take a taxi or a bus to reach the farms.

Finally, no exploration of Singapore's hidden gems would be complete without a visit to *Little India* and *Arab Street*, two vibrant areas that reflect the city's cultural diversity. *Little India* is known for its colorful streets, traditional Indian shops, and authentic Indian cuisine. One of the main attractions here is the Sri Veeramakaliamman Temple, a beautiful Hindu temple that is open to visitors. Walking through the streets of Little India, you'll find everything from flower garland shops to spice stalls and textile stores. It's also a fantastic place to try local dishes like roti prata, biryani, and dosas. Nearby, *Arab Street* is the center of Singapore's Muslim community, with the stunning Sultan Mosque as its focal point.

The streets around Arab Street are filled with Middle Eastern cafés, carpet shops, and boutiques selling traditional fabrics and clothing.

The area is also famous for its street art, especially along Haji Lane, making it a lively and colorful spot to explore. To get to Little India, take the MRT to Little India Station on the North-East Line. For Arab Street, you can alight at Bugis Station on the East-West Line or Downtown Line

However, Singapore's hidden gems provide a different perspective on the city, away from the modern skyline and bustling shopping districts. Whether you're exploring the quirky Haw Par Villa, cycling through the rustic landscapes of Pulau Ubin, walking the scenic Southern Ridges, or uncovering the rich heritage of Kampong Glam, Kranji, Little India, and Arab Street, each of these places offers a unique experience that showcases Singapore's cultural diversity and natural beauty.

These destinations are all easily accessible by public transport, making it simple to explore beyond the typical tourist trail and discover the hidden sides of Singapore.

CHAPTER 8

MUST DO HIKES AND TRAILS

Beyond its iconic skyscrapers and busy streets, this city surprises visitors with its lush green spaces and a variety of trails and hiking paths, perfect for those who love to explore the outdoors. Despite its small size, Singapore has a network of well-maintained nature reserves, parks, and islands where you can enjoy a range of hiking experiences, from easy, family-friendly walks to more challenging treks. These trails offer a great way to see a different side of Singapore, surrounded by greenery and natural beauty. Here are some of the best hikes and trails that visitors can enjoy.

MacRitchie Reservoir Park

MacRitchie Reservoir is one of the most popular spots for nature lovers in Singapore. The park features a range of trails that wind around the reservoir and through the surrounding forest.

One of the main attractions is the TreeTop Walk, a free-standing suspension bridge that offers a bird's-eye view of the forest canopy. The trails here range from short 3 km loops to longer 11 km routes, making it possible to choose how much time and energy you want to spend. It's a peaceful spot for wildlife spotting, where you might see monkeys, monitor lizards, and a variety of birds. To get there, take the MRT to *Caldecott Station* and then hop on a bus to the entrance of the park.

Southern Ridges

The Southern Ridges is a collection of trails that stretch over 10 kilometers, linking Mount Faber Park, Telok Blangah Hill Park, HortPark, Kent Ridge Park, and Labrador Nature Reserve. The route offers scenic views of the city skyline, harbor, and lush greenery. The Henderson Waves, a wave-shaped bridge, is one of the key highlights, offering great photo opportunities. The trails are mostly paved, making them accessible to walkers of all levels.

The Southern Ridges are perfect for those who want a mix of urban and natural scenery. You can start the trail from *Harbourfront MRT Station* near Mount Faber or at *Kent Ridge MRT Station*.

Bukit Timah Nature Reserve

Bukit Timah Nature Reserve is home to Singapore's tallest natural hill, Bukit Timah Hill, which stands at 163 meters. The trails here are steeper than others in the city, making it more challenging, but the effort is rewarded with a chance to see one of the last remaining areas of primary rainforest in Singapore. The main trail up the hill takes about 30 to 45 minutes, but there are also several side trails that take you deeper into the reserve. It's a popular spot for fitness enthusiasts who want a more intense workout. The nature reserve is accessible via *Beauty World MRT Station*.

Coney Island

Coney Island, located in the northeastern part of Singapore, is known for its rustic charm.

The island has several trails that take you along beaches, forests, and open fields. It's a great spot for those looking for an easy, flat hike, and it's also popular for cycling. Coney Island is relatively untouched, so you'll get a sense of what Singapore might have been like before it became a bustling metropolis. You can reach the island by taking the MRT to *Punggol Station* and then catching a bus to Punggol Point Park.

Pulau Ubin

For a truly rustic experience, take a trip to Pulau Ubin, a small island located to the northeast of Singapore. The island offers a glimpse of what life was like in Singapore in the 1960s, with its kampong (village) setting, dirt paths, and unspoiled nature. The trails here are suitable for walking and cycling, and one of the main attractions is the Chek Jawa Wetlands, where you can explore mangroves and see a variety of marine life.

Pulau Ubin is only a short boat ride away from Changi Point Ferry Terminal, giving you a quick escape from the city's hustle and bustle.

East Coast Park

East Coast Park is one of Singapore's most beloved parks, stretching over 15 kilometers along the southeastern coastline. It's ideal for those who want a long, leisurely walk by the sea. The park is also popular with joggers, cyclists, and families, offering numerous facilities, including barbecue pits, cafes, and rest areas. For a relaxing day, you can walk along the coast, rent a bicycle, or just enjoy the sea breeze. The park is accessible from *Bedok MRT Station* and *Mountbatten MRT Station*.

Labrador Nature Reserve

Labrador Nature Reserve is a coastal park that offers a blend of history, nature, and scenic sea views. It has several easy trails that take you past old British bunkers and tunnels, along with beautiful views of the harbor.

The park's coastal boardwalk is a highlight, providing a calm and relaxing walk with the sound of the waves. It's also a great spot for bird-watching. You can reach the park by taking the MRT to *Labrador Park Station*.

Sungei Buloh Wetland Reserve

For those interested in seeing more wildlife, Sungei Buloh Wetland Reserve is a fantastic spot for bird-watching. The trails here take you through mangroves, mudflats, and forests, offering a chance to see migratory birds, monitor lizards, mudskippers, and even crocodiles. The reserve is a bit out of the way, but it's worth the trip if you want to see a different side of Singapore's natural environment. You can get there by taking the MRT to *Kranji Station* and then taking a bus to the reserve.

These trails and nature spots provide a great way to see Singapore's green spaces and natural beauty. Whether you're looking for a challenging climb or a gentle stroll, there is a trail for every type of hiker.

Each of these locations is well-maintained, with clear paths and signs, making it easy for anyone to explore. Remember to bring plenty of water, wear comfortable shoes, and check the weather before you set out to ensure a safe and enjoyable hike.

CHAPTER 9

BUCKET LIST FOR SOLO TRAVELERS

When traveling solo, Singapore offers a wealth of experiences that cater perfectly to individual exploration. Whether you're wandering through cultural neighborhoods, enjoying a quiet moment in a park, or diving into the vibrant food scene, Singapore has something for every solo traveler. Here is a comprehensive bucket list that highlights some of the must-see attractions and hidden gems for those exploring Singapore alone.

One of the best places to start your solo adventure in Singapore is by visiting *Gardens by the Bay*. This expansive garden showcases the futuristic Supertree Grove, the Cloud Forest, and the Flower Dome.

The peaceful environment is perfect for solo travelers who want to take their time wandering through the green spaces while enjoying the spectacular views of nature and architecture blending seamlessly together. The Cloud Forest, with its indoor waterfall, provides a calm and cool atmosphere, making it an ideal place for a quiet stroll. Don't miss the OCBC Skyway, a walkway suspended between two Supertrees, where you can enjoy a breathtaking view of the gardens and the city. To get there, take the MRT to Bayfront Station (Circle Line or Downtown Line), and follow the signs for a short walk to the entrance.

For solo travelers who enjoy panoramic views, the *Marina Bay Sands SkyPark* is a must. Located on top of one of the most iconic buildings in Singapore, this observation deck offers stunning views of the city, including the Marina Bay area, the Singapore Flyer, and the bustling skyline. It's a great spot for solo travelers who love photography or simply want to relax and take in the view.

The SkyPark is also home to the world's highest rooftop infinity pool, but pool access is reserved for hotel guests. However, the observation deck alone makes the visit worthwhile. To reach Marina Bay Sands, take the MRT to Bayfront Station and follow the signs to the SkyPark.

A bucket list for solo travelers would not be complete without a visit to *Sentosa Island*. Sentosa is known as Singapore's island of fun and relaxation. It offers a wide range of attractions, including *Universal Studios Singapore*, sandy beaches, nature trails, and luxurious resorts. Whether you're seeking adventure or just some quiet time by the beach, Sentosa has it all. Solo travelers can enjoy visiting Universal Studios Singapore to experience thrilling rides or take a peaceful walk along scenic beaches like Siloso Beach or Palawan Beach. Sentosa is also home to the S.E.A. Aquarium and Adventure Cove Waterpark, making it a perfect spot for a full day of solo exploration.

Getting to Sentosa is easy—take the MRT to Harbourfront Station (North-East Line or Circle Line) and then board the Sentosa Express from VivoCity shopping mall, or take a scenic ride on the cable car from Mount Faber.

For a more cultural experience, *Chinatown* is a vibrant and historically rich neighborhood perfect for solo travelers looking to explore the city's heritage. Chinatown offers a mix of temples, traditional shops, and modern cafés. Visit the Buddha Tooth Relic Temple, a stunning Buddhist temple where you can learn about Singapore's religious history. If you're looking to sample local food, Chinatown Food Street is a great place to grab a bite. It's lined with hawker stalls serving Singaporean classics like char kway teow, chicken rice, and satay. The Chinatown Heritage Centre is another must-visit spot for those interested in learning more about the area's history. Chinatown is easily accessible by taking the MRT to Chinatown Station (North-East Line or Downtown Line).

For a touch of nature and peace, solo travelers should not miss *Pulau Ubin*, one of Singapore's last remaining rural areas. Pulau Ubin offers a rare opportunity to see what Singapore looked like before it became a modern city-state. You can rent a bicycle and explore the island's lush greenery, mangroves, and traditional kampong houses. One of the highlights is the Chek Jawa Wetlands, a beautiful nature reserve with a wide range of wildlife and plant species. The island is ideal for solo travelers who want to escape the city and experience Singapore's quieter, natural side. To get there, take a bumboat from Changi Point Ferry Terminal, which is a short bus ride from Tanah Merah MRT Station (East-West Line).

Another fantastic nature escape is *MacRitchie Reservoir Park*, which is perfect for solo travelers who love hiking and outdoor activities. The park features well-marked trails through Singapore's tropical rainforest, including the famous TreeTop Walk, a suspension bridge that offers stunning views of the forest canopy.

The serene environment is ideal for those seeking some alone time while being surrounded by nature. MacRitchie Reservoir is home to a variety of wildlife, including monkeys and birds, so you'll have plenty to see as you walk along the trails. To get there, take the MRT to Marymount Station (Circle Line), and then a short bus ride will take you to the entrance of the park.

Solo dining is an experience to be savored in Singapore, and one of the best places to do this is at a hawker center. Singapore's hawker centers are bustling food courts where you can find a wide variety of local dishes at affordable prices. *Maxwell Food Centre*, *Lau Pa Sat*, and *Old Airport Road Food Centre* are some of the top hawker centers where you can enjoy favorites like laksa, Hainanese chicken rice, and chili crab. Dining solo at a hawker center is easy, as the communal seating arrangements allow you to simply find a spot, order from your chosen stall, and enjoy the meal without the need for reservations or a table for two.

These centers are also great places to strike up a conversation with locals and learn more about Singaporean food culture. Maxwell Food Centre is a short walk from Chinatown MRT Station, Lau Pa Sat is near Raffles Place MRT Station, and Old Airport Road Food Centre can be reached via Dakota MRT Station (Circle Line).

For art and culture enthusiasts, a visit to the *National Gallery Singapore* is a must. This impressive gallery houses the largest public collection of modern art in Southeast Asia and is a great spot for solo travelers who enjoy exploring art at their own pace. The gallery is located in two beautifully restored historical buildings, the former Supreme Court and City Hall, making it as much a cultural experience as an artistic one. Solo travelers can wander through the various exhibitions, learning about Singaporean and Southeast Asian art in a quiet, reflective environment. The National Gallery is located in the Civic District and can be reached by taking the MRT to City Hall Station (North-South Line or East-West Line).

If you enjoy shopping, make sure to include *Haji Lane* on your solo travel bucket list. This quirky street in Kampong Glam is known for its eclectic mix of independent boutiques, vibrant street art, and cafés. It's the perfect place to spend a few hours exploring shops that sell everything from handmade jewelry to unique clothing and home décor. The colorful murals along the lane also make for great photo opportunities. After shopping, you can relax in one of the trendy cafés and enjoy a coffee or a snack. Haji Lane is located near Bugis MRT Station (East-West Line or Downtown Line), making it easy to reach.

Finally, for solo travelers who want to experience Singapore's nightlife, *Clarke Quay* is the place to be. Clarke Quay is a riverside district known for its lively bars, clubs, and restaurants. It's a great place for solo travelers to enjoy an evening drink, take a boat ride along the Singapore River, or simply soak up the vibrant atmosphere. Many of the bars offer live music, and the area is filled with people enjoying the nightlife.

Whether you prefer a quiet rooftop bar or a lively club, Clarke Quay has something for everyone. To get there, take the MRT to Clarke Quay Station (North-East Line).

However, Singapore offers a wealth of experiences for solo travelers, from cultural exploration and nature walks to great food and shopping. Each of these destinations is easily accessible by public transport, making it convenient for solo travelers to explore the city at their own pace. Whether you're visiting Gardens by the Bay, dining at a hawker center, or enjoying a peaceful moment at MacRitchie Reservoir, Singapore is a city that caters to every type of solo traveler.

CHAPTER 10

BUCKET LIST FOR COUPLES

Singapore is a fantastic destination for couples looking to experience a blend of culture, modern attractions, and intimate moments. Whether you're seeking romantic walks, luxurious dining, or exciting adventures, the city has plenty to offer. From stunning views to serene nature escapes, Singapore provides a mix of activities that allow couples to bond and make memories together. Here's a look at some romantic activities and places for couples to explore in Singapore.

One of the most iconic places for couples to visit is *Gardens by the Bay*, where you can immerse yourselves in lush greenery and futuristic architecture.

The *Supertree Grove* is a highlight, featuring towering tree-like structures that come alive with lights and music during the nightly Garden Rhapsody show. This light show creates a magical atmosphere, perfect for a romantic evening stroll. The *Cloud Forest* is another must-see within the gardens, offering a peaceful and cool retreat with its misty mountain and indoor waterfall. If you're both nature lovers, the *Flower Dome* will take you on a journey through a variety of plants and flowers from all over the world. To add to the romance, take a walk on the OCBC Skyway, a suspended bridge that gives you a panoramic view of the gardens and beyond. To get there, take the MRT to Bayfront Station (Circle Line or Downtown Line) and follow the signs to Gardens by the Bay.

For couples seeking luxury and breathtaking views, *Marina Bay Sands SkyPark* is the perfect spot.

This observation deck, located on top of the famous Marina Bay Sands Hotel, offers one of the best views of Singapore's skyline.

From here, you can enjoy stunning views of the city, Marina Bay, and even neighboring countries on a clear day. It's an ideal location for couples who want to take memorable photos or simply enjoy the view together. If you're feeling indulgent, you can stay at the Marina Bay Sands Hotel and experience the rooftop infinity pool, known for its incredible views over the city. Even if you're not staying at the hotel, SkyPark's observation deck is worth a visit. To reach Marina Bay Sands, take the MRT to Bayfront Station, which is directly connected to the hotel.

For an unforgettable island escape, *Sentosa Island* is a must on any couple's bucket list. Known for its mix of adventure and relaxation, Sentosa offers something for every kind of couple. For those seeking thrills, *Universal Studios Singapore* provides a day of fun with exciting rides and entertainment.

If you prefer a more relaxing day, the island's beaches, such as *Siloso Beach* and *Palawan Beach*, are perfect for unwinding together by the sea. Couples can also enjoy a romantic cable car ride from Mount Faber to Sentosa, offering panoramic views of the city and the island. In the evening, head to *Wings of Time*, a mesmerizing outdoor night show featuring water, lasers, and pyrotechnics that tells a story of friendship and adventure. To get to Sentosa, take the MRT to Harbourfront Station (North-East Line or Circle Line), and from there, you can board the Sentosa Express monorail or take the cable car from Mount Faber.

For couples who enjoy cultural experiences, *Chinatown* is a great place to explore hand in hand. Chinatown is one of Singapore's most historic and vibrant neighborhoods, offering a mix of traditional temples, bustling markets, and charming streets. Visit the *Buddha Tooth Relic Temple*, a beautiful temple where you can learn about Buddhist culture while enjoying the peaceful atmosphere.

If you're both food lovers, Chinatown Food Street is a perfect spot to sample local dishes like char kway teow, chicken rice, and satay. It's a great way to bond over Singapore's rich culinary heritage. After exploring the area, head to *Ann Siang Hill*, a quieter street lined with stylish restaurants and bars, ideal for a romantic dinner or drinks. To reach Chinatown, take the MRT to Chinatown Station (North-East Line or Downtown Line).

For a romantic day in nature, couples should not miss a trip to *MacRitchie Reservoir*. This park is a haven for nature lovers and provides plenty of opportunities for couples to enjoy a peaceful hike or canoeing. One of the park's highlights is the *TreeTop Walk*, a suspension bridge that offers a bird's-eye view of the tropical rainforest. The serene surroundings make it a perfect place to escape the city's bustle and reconnect with nature. You can also take a picnic along the reservoir's peaceful trails, creating a quiet, romantic moment amid nature.

To get to MacRitchie Reservoir, take the MRT to Marymount Station (Circle Line), and from there, it's a short bus ride to the park entrance.

If you prefer a more relaxed and slow-paced experience, a stroll through *Singapore Botanic Gardens* is an ideal choice for couples. The Botanic Gardens are a UNESCO World Heritage Site and provide a beautiful backdrop for a romantic walk. The *National Orchid Garden*, located within the gardens, is a must-visit, showcasing over 1,000 species and 2,000 hybrids of orchids. Couples can enjoy the colorful flowers and quiet paths, making it an ideal spot for both nature and photography lovers. The gardens also have plenty of shaded benches where you can sit together and enjoy the peaceful surroundings. To reach Singapore Botanic Gardens, take the MRT to Botanic Gardens Station (Circle Line or Downtown Line).

For a unique and relaxing evening, couples can enjoy a romantic river cruise along the *Singapore River*.

The *Singapore River Cruise* takes you through the heart of the city, passing by iconic landmarks such as Clarke Quay, Boat Quay, and the Marina Bay area. The cruise is especially beautiful at night when the city lights reflect off the water, creating a magical atmosphere. It's a peaceful way to experience the city from a different perspective, and the slow pace of the boat ride allows you to relax and take in the sights together. River cruises typically start from Clarke Quay, which can be reached via the MRT (North-East Line) at Clarke Quay Station.

If you're looking for a culinary adventure, Singapore's rooftop dining scene offers incredible views and romantic settings. *Ce La Vi*, located on top of Marina Bay Sands, provides panoramic views of the city and a perfect setting for a romantic dinner or drinks. For couples who want to experience fine dining with a view, *1-Altitude* is another fantastic option.

Located at 282 meters above ground, 1-Altitude is one of the world's highest alfresco bars and offers breathtaking views of Singapore's skyline, perfect for a memorable night out. Both venues offer a luxurious dining experience with a range of cocktails and gourmet dishes, making them ideal spots for couples looking to indulge.

However, Singapore offers an abundance of experiences for couples, from scenic nature walks and cultural explorations to luxurious dining and romantic island getaways. Each experience is designed to bring couples closer together, creating unforgettable memories while exploring the best that Singapore has to offer. With its rich variety of activities, stunning landscapes, and vibrant cityscape, Singapore is truly a destination that caters to couples seeking adventure, relaxation, and everything in between. Whether you're watching the sunset from Marina Bay Sands SkyPark or walking hand in hand through the Botanic Gardens, Singapore is a city that invites couples to experience its beauty together.

CHAPTER 11
BUCKET LIST FOR FAMILY WITH KIDS

Traveling with kids in Singapore is an exciting and enriching experience. The city is filled with family-friendly activities that cater to children of all ages, offering a mix of fun, adventure, learning, and nature. Whether your family enjoys thrilling rides, animal encounters, or hands-on science exhibits, Singapore has plenty of attractions that will keep both kids and parents entertained. The city's efficient transport system makes getting to these attractions easy, so you can plan your day without worrying about logistics. A great starting point for families is *Sentosa Island*, Singapore's dedicated island resort filled with fun attractions for children and adults alike.

One of the top spots on Sentosa is *Universal Studios Singapore*, a theme park that brings favorite movie characters and exciting rides to life.

With seven different zones, including Hollywood, New York, and Madagascar, there's something for every member of the family. Younger children will love the kid-friendly rides, while older kids and parents can enjoy thrilling roller coasters like Battlestar Galactica. There are also live shows, parades, and opportunities to meet characters like Shrek and the Minions, making it a day of fun for the whole family. Getting to Sentosa is easy; take the MRT to Harbourfront Station (North-East Line or Circle Line), and from there, you can either take the Sentosa Express monorail or the cable car for a more scenic arrival.

For a mix of education and entertainment, *Singapore's Science Centre* is a must-visit for families. This interactive museum is perfect for kids who love learning through hands-on exhibits. The Science Centre covers a wide range of topics, including biology, physics, and space exploration, with plenty of interactive displays that allow children to explore and experiment.

One of the highlights for families is the *Butterfly Garden* and *Omni-Theatre*, where you can watch immersive dome films about space and nature. During school holidays, the Science Centre also hosts special workshops and demonstrations that are fun and educational. The Science Centre is located in Jurong and can be reached by taking the MRT to Jurong East Station (East-West Line), followed by a short bus ride.

Animal lovers will enjoy spending time at the *Singapore Zoo*, one of the best family-friendly destinations in the city. The zoo is known for its open-concept design, where animals roam in naturalistic habitats that closely mimic their environments. Children will love seeing animals like orangutans, elephants, and lions up close, and the *Rainforest Kidzworld* area offers water play and farm animal interactions, which are always a hit with younger visitors.

The zoo also offers special experiences like feeding sessions, where kids can feed animals like giraffes and elephants under the guidance of the zoo staff. If your family enjoys animals, you can extend your visit to include the *River Wonders* and *Night Safari*, both located next to the zoo. The Night Safari is a unique experience that allows families to explore the zoo after dark, where nocturnal animals come to life in their natural habitats. To reach the zoo, take the MRT to Khatib Station (North-South Line), and then take the Mandai Khatib Shuttle to the zoo.

Another great option for families is *Gardens by the Bay*, a beautiful outdoor space that offers a mix of nature and play areas for children. The *Children's Garden* within Gardens by the Bay is designed specifically for kids, with water play areas, treehouses, and climbing structures that allow children to run around and enjoy the outdoors. The water play area is especially popular on hot days, and it's a great way for kids to cool down while having fun.

Beyond the Children's Garden, the *Supertree Grove* and *Flower Dome* are also worth exploring, as they offer stunning views and colorful plants from around the world. Gardens by the Bay can be reached via Bayfront MRT Station (Circle Line or Downtown Line), and the Children's Garden is located within the larger garden complex.

For a day of fun and adventure, families should visit *Adventure Cove Waterpark* on Sentosa Island. This waterpark offers thrilling water slides, a lazy river, and snorkeling opportunities in a tropical setting. The park is perfect for both younger children and teens, with attractions like the *Rainbow Reef*, where kids can snorkel and see tropical fish up close. Adventure Cove also has a wave pool and splash areas, making it a fun destination for families to enjoy water activities together. Since Adventure Cove is on Sentosa Island, getting there is the same as for Universal Studios Singapore—take the MRT to Harbourfront Station and then transfer to the Sentosa Express or cable car.

Another family favorite is the *Singapore Flyer*, Asia's largest observation wheel. This is a great way for families to see the city from above, with breathtaking views of Marina Bay, the Singapore River, and even parts of Malaysia and Indonesia on clear days. The enclosed capsules are spacious and safe, making it easy for families to enjoy the ride together. The experience lasts about 30 minutes, and kids will love spotting landmarks from high up in the sky. The Singapore Flyer is located near the Marina Bay area and is accessible by taking the MRT to Promenade Station (Circle Line).

For a taste of culture and history that's still fun for kids, a visit to *Fort Canning Park* offers both education and exploration. The park is home to the *Battlebox*, an underground bunker used during World War II, which has been turned into an interactive museum that teaches kids about Singapore's wartime history. The park itself is filled with lush greenery and offers plenty of space for children to run around, making it a great spot for a family picnic or stroll.

Fort Canning Park is also home to special events and festivals throughout the year, adding extra excitement for families. You can reach Fort Canning Park by taking the MRT to Fort Canning Station (Downtown Line).

Finally, if your family enjoys nature and wildlife, a visit to *Jurong Bird Park* is a wonderful way to spend the day. The park is home to over 5,000 birds from around the world, including flamingos, parrots, and penguins. One of the highlights for families is the *Lory Loft*, where kids can feed colorful lories and interact with the birds up close. The park also features bird shows and exhibits that teach children about bird conservation and the importance of protecting wildlife. To get to Jurong Bird Park, take the MRT to Boon Lay Station (East-West Line), and from there, a short bus ride will take you to the park entrance.

However, Singapore offers a wide range of family-friendly activities that make traveling with kids enjoyable and stress-free.

From the exciting rides at Universal Studios and Adventure Cove to the educational experiences at the Science Centre and Singapore Zoo, there is something for every family to enjoy. The city's convenient public transport system makes getting to these attractions easy, ensuring that you can plan your day without any hassle. Whether you're spending time outdoors at Gardens by the Bay or exploring the cultural history of Fort Canning Park, Singapore is filled with kid-friendly adventures that are sure to create lasting memories for the entire family.

CHAPTER 12

BUCKET LIST FOR GROUP

Traveling with a group in Singapore opens up a world of exciting opportunities and unique experiences. Whether you're planning an adventure with friends, a family gathering, or a corporate team-building trip, Singapore offers plenty of activities that are perfect for large groups. The city is designed with excellent infrastructure and services, making it easy for groups to navigate and enjoy everything from thrilling adventures to relaxed dining experiences together. Here's a look at some of the best activities and services that cater specifically to group travelers in Singapore.

For large groups looking for a well-organized experience, booking *Best Tours and Activities for Large Groups* is an ideal way to explore the city without the hassle of planning every detail.

Singapore has several tour companies that offer customized group tours, whether your interests are focused on culture, nature, or city sightseeing. A great option for group travel is the *Chinatown Heritage Tour*, which guides you through the historic streets, temples, and markets of Chinatown, offering a glimpse into Singapore's rich cultural past. These tours can be tailored to include special stops, and you can arrange private guides to ensure the tour is exclusive to your group. For those who want a more relaxed experience, the *Singapore River Cruise* is another group-friendly option. These cruises take you past iconic landmarks like Marina Bay Sands, the Merlion, and Clarke Quay, allowing the entire group to sit back, enjoy the scenery, and learn about the city's history. Cruises can be booked for private group tours, ensuring that your party has the boat to themselves. Most of these tours start from MRT-accessible locations like Clarke Quay or Chinatown.

If your group prefers a more customized experience, consider arranging *private group tours and guides*.

These private tours allow you to explore the city with a dedicated guide who can adapt the itinerary to suit your group's preferences. Whether you want to focus on Singapore's colonial history, explore the modern architecture of Marina Bay, or dive into the local food scene, a private guide can ensure that your group sees the best of the city without the crowds. Private transportation can also be arranged, making it convenient for groups to move between attractions. Popular tour operators offer services that start from key tourist hubs, with pickups available from major hotels or directly from places like Changi Airport. With a private guide, your group can explore at its own pace and enjoy a more intimate travel experience.

For groups seeking adventure, Singapore offers a wide range of *adventure sports* that are perfect for a day of excitement and bonding. One of the most thrilling activities is *indoor skydiving at iFly Singapore* on Sentosa Island. This indoor skydiving facility allows groups to experience the sensation of free-falling in a safe, controlled environment.

It's a great way for groups to enjoy an adrenaline rush together, and iFly offers packages that accommodate large groups. Another popular activity is *cable skiing at Singapore Wake Park*, located at East Coast Park. Here, participants are pulled by a cable system while wakeboarding across a lagoon. The park caters to all skill levels, so both beginners and experienced riders in your group can enjoy the fun. If your group prefers something more grounded but equally exciting, head to *Mega Adventure Park* in Sentosa for a day of ziplining. The park's MegaZip lets you soar 450 meters across the jungle canopy, with panoramic views of the ocean below. These adventure sports are designed with safety in mind and provide a thrilling experience for groups looking to try something new.

For corporate groups or those traveling for team-building purposes, Singapore offers a variety of *team-building activities* that focus on cooperation, problem-solving, and fun.

Many companies specialize in creating unique team-building experiences, such as treasure hunts, escape room challenges, and outdoor adventure courses. One of the most popular venues for team-building activities is *Forest Adventure*, an outdoor obstacle course located at Bedok Reservoir. Groups can navigate through a series of high ropes, zip lines, and bridges, working together to complete the course. Another option is *Sentosa's Amazing Race*, where groups compete in a series of physical and mental challenges spread across Sentosa Island. These activities are designed to encourage communication, teamwork, and leadership skills, making them ideal for corporate outings or large groups of friends looking to bond. To reach Forest Adventure, take the MRT to Bedok Station, and a short bus ride will take you to Bedok Reservoir.

Of course, no group trip is complete without good food, and Singapore offers plenty of *dining options for groups*, with restaurants that cater to large parties and offer special group menus.

For those looking to indulge in a wide variety of dishes, buffets are an excellent choice. One of the best buffet restaurants for groups is *The Line* at Shangri-La Hotel, which offers a huge selection of international cuisine, including Asian, Western, and seafood options. The restaurant's spacious layout and group-friendly seating make it perfect for large gatherings. If your group prefers a more intimate dining experience, many restaurants in Singapore offer *group menus* designed for sharing. Places like *Din Tai Fung* (famous for its dumplings) and *No Signboard Seafood* (known for its chili crab) are great options, as they provide dishes that can be shared family-style, ensuring that everyone can try a variety of local flavors. For groups looking to celebrate a special occasion, many restaurants also offer *event spaces* that can be reserved for private dining. These spaces are ideal for birthday celebrations, corporate dinners, or any special event where your group wants a more personalized experience.

Finally, Singapore is a fantastic destination for group travel, with a wide variety of activities that cater to large parties. Whether you're exploring the city on a private tour, enjoying thrilling adventure sports, participating in team-building challenges, or dining together at one of Singapore's many group-friendly restaurants, there is something for everyone to enjoy. The city's efficient transportation system and well-organized attractions make it easy to plan and manage group activities, ensuring a smooth and enjoyable experience for all. With so many options available, Singapore is sure to provide your group with an unforgettable adventure.

CHAPTER 13

BUCKET LIST FOR ADVENTURE SEEKERS

For those who love a bit of thrill and excitement, Singapore offers plenty of adventurous activities that go beyond the usual city experience. Whether you're diving into the nocturnal world of animals, exploring underwater realms, or pushing your limits with adrenaline-pumping sports, Singapore has something for every adventure seeker. With an exciting blend of outdoor activities, extreme sports, and nature exploration, there's no shortage of options for those looking to add a bit of adventure to their trip.

One of the most exhilarating and unique adventures in Singapore is the *Night Safari at the Singapore Zoo*. This world-renowned experience allows you to explore a wildlife park after dark, offering a rare glimpse into the lives of nocturnal animals.

Unlike traditional zoos, the Night Safari is designed to let animals roam in habitats that closely mimic their natural environments, so you get to see creatures like leopards, tigers, and elephants at their most active. You can start your night with the tram ride, which takes you through different zones or opt for a walking trail where you can explore the park at your own pace. It's a thrilling yet educational way to experience wildlife, perfect for anyone looking to combine adventure with nature. To get there, take the MRT to Khatib Station (North-South Line) and catch the Mandai Khatib Shuttle to the zoo.

For those who prefer underwater exploration, Singapore offers *scuba diving and snorkeling experiences* that allow you to dive into a world of vibrant marine life. One of the best places to explore is *Pulau Hantu*, a small island off the coast of Singapore. Despite its name, which translates to "Ghost Island," Pulau Hantu is popular for its rich marine biodiversity. Scuba diving here gives you the chance to see coral reefs, seahorses, and even turtles.

If you're new to diving, there are diving schools in Singapore that offer courses and guided dives, making it accessible for beginners. For those who prefer something less intense, snorkeling is also a great option and allows you to enjoy the colorful underwater world at a slower pace. To get to Pulau Hantu, you'll need to take a boat from West Coast Pier, which can be reached by a short bus ride from Clementi MRT Station (East-West Line).

Singapore is also a fantastic destination for *water sports*, with activities like wakeboarding, kayaking, and paddleboarding available for thrill-seekers. *East Coast Park* is one of the best spots for water activities, offering a variety of options for different skill levels. If you've never tried wakeboarding before, there are schools at East Coast Park that offer lessons and equipment rental. The calm waters along the coastline are perfect for kayaking and paddleboarding, allowing you to enjoy the sea while testing your balance and strength.

For those looking for something more intense, head to *Sentosa's Wave House* for an exciting flow-rider experience, where you can try your hand at surfing simulated waves in a controlled environment. East Coast Park is easily accessible via the MRT; take the East-West Line to Bedok Station and then a bus to the park.

For adrenaline junkies, Singapore offers a range of extreme sports that are sure to get your heart racing. *Bungy Jumping at AJ Hackett* on Sentosa Island is one of the top experiences for thrill-seekers. At a height of 50 meters, this bungy jump lets you take a daring leap with views of the beach below. If jumping isn't your style but you still want an adrenaline rush, you can try the *Giant Swing*, also located at AJ Hackett, which swings you and a friend through the air at high speeds. Another must-try for adventure enthusiasts is *indoor skydiving at iFly Singapore*, also on Sentosa.

iFly allows you to experience the sensation of free-falling without jumping out of a plane, making it a perfect option for those who want the thrill of skydiving in a controlled environment. Both AJ Hackett and iFly are located on Sentosa Island, which can be reached via the MRT at Harbourfront Station, followed by the Sentosa Express or cable car.

For those who love outdoor exploration, *Singapore's best hiking and biking trails* offer a combination of natural beauty and adventure. The *Southern Ridges* is a 10-kilometer trail that connects parks and green spaces like Mount Faber, HortPark, and Kent Ridge Park. The highlight of the Southern Ridges is the *Henderson Waves*, Singapore's highest pedestrian bridge, offering panoramic views of the forest and city. The trail is perfect for both hiking and biking, with well-maintained paths that make the journey enjoyable for all levels. Another great spot for hiking is *MacRitchie Reservoir*, home to the famous *TreeTop Walk*.

This suspension bridge takes you through the forest canopy, providing breathtaking views of the surrounding greenery. For those who prefer cycling, the *Eastern Coastal Loop* is a popular biking trail that stretches along the coast, providing scenic views and plenty of fresh sea air. The Southern Ridges can be accessed from Mount Faber, near Harbourfront MRT Station, while MacRitchie Reservoir is accessible via Marymount MRT Station.

Finally, Singapore is an adventure seeker's paradise with a wide array of thrilling activities both on land and in the water. Whether you're exploring wildlife at night, diving into the ocean, or tackling a challenging hike, the city offers endless opportunities for excitement. With easy access to these adventure hotspots via Singapore's efficient transport system, getting your adrenaline fix has never been easier. From the heights of bungy jumping to the depths of scuba diving, Singapore is sure to provide unforgettable experiences for those who crave adventure.

CHAPTER 14

TOP RESTAURANT

Food is an essential part of the travel experience, and Singapore offers a vast array of restaurants catering to every type of traveler. Whether you're looking to enjoy affordable local flavors, explore family-friendly spots, or indulge in a luxurious dining experience, Singapore has it all. The city's rich cultural diversity means that food here reflects a blend of traditions, offering everything from humble hawker stalls to high-end gourmet restaurants.

Budget Travelers

For budget travelers, Singapore's hawker centers are unbeatable when it comes to affordable and delicious food. One of the most popular options is *Maxwell Food Centre* in Chinatown, known for its variety of local dishes.

Here, you can try Hainanese chicken rice, laksa, and other Singaporean staples without breaking the bank. One of the must-try stalls is Tian Tian Hainanese Chicken Rice, which has gained international fame for its tender chicken and fragrant rice. The casual, bustling environment makes it a great spot for travelers who want to experience authentic local flavors at wallet-friendly prices. To get there, take the MRT to Chinatown Station (North-East Line or Downtown Line), and Maxwell Food Centre is just a short walk away.

Another fantastic option for budget-conscious travelers is *Old Airport Road Food Centre*, one of Singapore's oldest and largest hawker centers. With over 150 stalls, it offers a wide range of affordable dishes, including char kway teow (fried flat noodles), satay, and prawn mee (prawn noodles). For travelers who enjoy trying a variety of foods, Old Airport Road is a must-visit. One of the well-loved stalls here is Lao Fu Zi Fried Kway Teow, famous for its smoky and flavorful noodle dish.

To get there, take the MRT to Dakota Station (Circle Line), and the food center is a short walk away.

Family with Kids Travelers

For families traveling with kids, dining in Singapore is easy thanks to the numerous family-friendly restaurants that cater to young diners with kids' menus, high chairs, and spacious seating. *Jumbo Seafood* is a family favorite, especially for those looking to try Singapore's famous chili crab. With several locations across the city, including a waterfront spot at East Coast Park, it's an excellent place for families to gather and enjoy a meal. The restaurant offers a comfortable setting, and the large tables make it ideal for families. Jumbo's signature chili crab is a must-try, along with other seafood options like black pepper crab and cereal prawns. To visit the East Coast Park location, take the MRT to Bedok Station (East-West Line), and from there, it's a short bus or taxi ride to the park.

Another great option for families is *Slappy Cakes*, located at the Grandstand in Bukit Timah. This interactive dining experience allows children (and adults!) to make their pancakes right at the table, choosing from a variety of batters, toppings, and sauces. The hands-on experience is fun for kids, and the restaurant also offers a full menu with savory dishes and breakfast options. The casual and playful environment makes it perfect for families with young children. To get there, take the MRT to Botanic Gardens Station (Circle Line), and from there, you can catch a bus or taxi to the Grandstand.

Luxury Travelers

For luxury travelers seeking an upscale dining experience, Singapore is home to some of the finest restaurants in the world. *Odette*, a Michelin three-star restaurant located in the National Gallery, offers a modern French menu created by acclaimed chef Julien Royer. The elegant setting, combined with the artistic presentation of the dishes, makes dining here an unforgettable experience.

Odette is known for its seasonal menus that highlight fresh, premium ingredients sourced from around the world. The dining experience is refined, and the service is impeccable, making it ideal for special occasions or romantic dinners. To get there, take the MRT to City Hall Station (North-South Line or East-West Line), and the National Gallery is a short walk away.

Another top restaurant for luxury travelers is *Burnt Ends*, a Michelin-starred modern Australian barbecue restaurant located in Chinatown. Burnt Ends is famous for its open-concept kitchen, where diners can watch the chefs grill and roast meats, seafood, and vegetables in a custom-made wood-fired oven. The restaurant's signature dishes, like the pulled pork sanger and beef marmalade, are must-tries. Burnt Ends offers a lively and intimate dining atmosphere, perfect for travelers who appreciate high-quality food in a casual yet chic setting. To get there, take the MRT to Outram Park Station (East-West Line or North-East Line), and it's a short walk from the station.

Solo Travelers

For solo travelers who want to enjoy a good meal in a relaxed and comfortable setting, Singapore has plenty of options that cater to individual diners. *The Public Izakaya* at Tanjong Pagar is a great spot for solo travelers looking to enjoy Japanese food in a casual atmosphere. This izakaya (Japanese-style pub) offers a wide range of small plates, from grilled skewers to sashimi, that are perfect for solo diners. The bar seating and laid-back vibe make it easy to enjoy a meal on your own while soaking in the lively ambiance. To get there, take the MRT to Tanjong Pagar Station (East-West Line), and the izakaya is located just a short walk away.

Another good option for solo travelers is *Tiong Bahru Bakery*, a cozy café located in the trendy Tiong Bahru neighborhood. Known for its freshly baked croissants and artisanal coffee, this bakery is an excellent place for solo travelers to relax and enjoy a quiet breakfast or lunch.

The relaxed vibe, coupled with comfortable seating, makes it a great spot to read a book or simply people-watch. To get there, take the MRT to Tiong Bahru Station (East-West Line), and the bakery is located nearby.

Vegetarian and Vegan Travelers

For vegetarian and vegan travelers, Singapore has a growing number of restaurants that offer delicious plant-based meals. *Afterglow by Anglow*, located in Chinatown, is a popular choice for those seeking fresh, plant-based dishes in a trendy setting. The restaurant focuses on locally sourced ingredients and serves a menu that includes raw and cooked vegan dishes, such as zucchini linguine, raw lasagna, and vegan cheese platters. Afterglow is known for its creative take on healthy, nutritious food, and the laid-back atmosphere makes it a great place to enjoy a meal with friends or solo. To get there, take the MRT to Chinatown Station (North-East Line or Downtown Line).

Another excellent option for vegetarian and vegan travelers is *Joie by Dozo*, located at Orchard Central. Joie offers a fine dining experience with a focus on modern meatless cuisine. The restaurant's set menus feature innovative dishes that use fresh vegetables, fruits, and plant-based ingredients, creating a dining experience that is both visually stunning and delicious. Joie is a great choice for travelers who want to indulge in a vegetarian meal while enjoying views of the city from the rooftop of Orchard Central. To get there, take the MRT to Somerset Station (North-South Line), and the restaurant is located within Orchard Central.

However, Singapore offers a diverse dining scene that caters to every type of traveler, whether you're on a budget, traveling with family, seeking luxury, or dining solo. With its wide range of restaurants, from local hawker centers to fine dining establishments, Singapore ensures that every meal is an experience to remember.

No matter where you choose to dine, the city's efficient public transport system makes it easy to get to your destination and enjoy the best food Singapore has to offer.

CHAPTER 15

WHERE TO TAKE PHOTOGRAPHS FOR MEMORIES

Taking photographs while visiting Singapore allows you to capture moments that will bring your trip to life long after it ends. Singapore is full of unique spots for photography, blending modern architecture, lush green spaces, and historic neighborhoods. Whether you're a casual traveler or a serious photography enthusiast, the city offers a wide variety of photogenic settings, each with its character and atmosphere.

One of the best locations for panoramic views of the city is Marina Bay Sands. The SkyPark Observation Deck, located on the rooftop of Marina Bay Sands, provides sweeping views of the Singapore skyline, including landmarks like the Singapore Flyer and Gardens by the Bay.

The view is particularly striking at sunset when the lights across the city begin to illuminate the skyline. Marina Bay Sands is easily accessible by taking the MRT to Bayfront Station.

Gardens by the Bay is another fantastic spot for both day and night photography. The Supertree Grove, with its towering tree-like structures, is a popular choice, especially during the evening light show when the Supertrees light up with colors. Within the gardens, the Flower Dome and Cloud Forest Domes offer interesting subjects for nature and landscape photos. You can reach Gardens by the Bay from Bayfront Station.

For a more traditional and colorful setting, Chinatown offers a wonderful opportunity to photograph heritage buildings, temples, and bustling market scenes. The Buddha Tooth Relic Temple and the Sri Mariamman Temple stand out with their beautiful architecture and cultural significance, making them ideal spots for capturing Singapore's multicultural heritage.

The markets, food stalls, and detailed facades in Chinatown add vibrant colors and textures to any photo. Chinatown can be reached by taking the MRT to Chinatown Station.

Little India is another vibrant district, perfect for capturing Singapore's rich cultural diversity. Here, the Sri Veeramakaliamman Temple and Tekka Market offer a lively backdrop filled with color and intricate architectural details. For the best light, visit in the morning or late afternoon when the colors are most vibrant. Little India is easily accessible from Little India Station.

For a modern and artistic atmosphere, head to Haji Lane in Kampong Glam. This narrow street is famous for its street art, small cafes, and eclectic shops, providing a trendy and colorful setting. The murals along Haji Lane make perfect backdrops, while the nearby Sultan Mosque adds a touch of historic beauty to the area. Haji Lane is accessible from Bugis Station.

Nature lovers should consider MacRitchie Reservoir and the Southern Ridges. The TreeTop Walk at MacRitchie is a suspension bridge over the rainforest, offering wide views of the lush surroundings. The Southern Ridges include the Henderson Waves Bridge, an architectural marvel that connects several parks. Both locations are ideal for early morning shots, with soft lighting and fewer visitors.

Sentosa Island offers beautiful beaches and tropical settings, including Palawan Beach and Tanjong Beach, with clear waters, sandy shores, and palm trees. Fort Siloso Skywalk also provides a unique view over Sentosa, making it a great option for capturing landscapes. Sentosa is easy to reach via the Sentosa Express from Harbourfront Station.

For a moving perspective of the city, the Singapore Flyer offers stunning views of Marina Bay and the city skyline, especially in the evening when the city lights create a beautiful backdrop.

The slow rotation of the Flyer allows for unique angles and time to capture each view. The Singapore Flyer is located near Marina Bay and can be accessed via Promenade Station.

If you're interested in working with a professional photographer, Singapore has many talented individuals specializing in travel and portrait photography. Photographers such as Darren Soh, known for his work with Singapore's urban landscapes, and Bryan van der Beek, recognized for his travel and portrait work, offer services that include guided photography tours. This is an option for travelers wanting personalized photo sessions or tips on capturing Singapore's sights.

With these locations and tips, you'll be able to capture the diversity and beauty of Singapore, from its bustling neighborhoods to its peaceful green spaces. Every corner of the city offers a new perspective, allowing you to create memories through photos that will remind you of your journey for years to come.

CHAPTER 16

SHOPPING AND SOUVENIRS

Shopping in Singapore is a truly exciting experience, offering a wide variety of choices for every type of shopper. Whether you're looking for luxury brands, unique local products, electronics, or traditional crafts, Singapore has it all. From world-famous shopping districts to hidden markets and specialty stores, you can find something to suit your style, interests, and budget. Shopping is not just about buying things in Singapore; it's about experiencing the city's vibrant culture, discovering its modern and historical areas, and enjoying the diversity of goods available. In this guide, we'll explore some of the top shopping spots that you should include in your Singapore travel itinerary, and we'll provide helpful details about how to get there and what to expect.

Orchard Road is probably the first place that comes to mind when people think about shopping in Singapore. This 2.2-kilometer stretch is the city's most famous shopping destination, filled with high-end stores, malls, and department stores. You'll find everything from luxury brands like Louis Vuitton and Chanel to more affordable fashion options like Zara and H&M. *ION Orchard* is one of the most iconic malls on Orchard Road, with an impressive collection of luxury and mid-range brands. It also has a wide range of restaurants, cafés, and even an art gallery, making it a destination in itself. For travelers seeking a mix of luxury and high-street brands, Orchard Road has plenty to offer. To get there, you can take the MRT to *Orchard Station* (North-South Line), which is located right in the heart of the shopping district.

For those looking to explore more affordable and unique shopping options, *Bugis Street Market* is the place to go. Bugis Street is one of the largest and cheapest shopping areas in Singapore, making it a favorite spot for tourists and locals alike.

Here, you can find everything from trendy clothes and accessories to souvenirs and local snacks. The vibrant atmosphere, with its bustling stalls and lively energy, gives Bugis Street a more market-like feel compared to the upscale malls. It's also a great place to pick up gifts or souvenirs to take home. The market offers affordable prices, and you can often find bargains if you're willing to explore the many different stalls. To reach Bugis Street, take the MRT to *Bugis Station* (East-West Line or Downtown Line), and the market is just a short walk away.

For travelers interested in electronics, gadgets, and tech accessories, *Sim Lim Square* is a well-known hub for all things tech-related. It's a multi-level mall dedicated to electronics, where you can find everything from the latest smartphones and cameras to computer parts and gaming gear. Sim Lim Square is particularly popular among tech enthusiasts looking for good deals or hard-to-find electronics.

However, it's important to note that prices and quality can vary between vendors, so it's always a good idea to compare prices and ensure you're buying from a reputable seller. Sim Lim Square is located near Bugis, and you can get there by taking the MRT to *Rochor Station* (Downtown Line).

For a more cultural and historical shopping experience, head to *Chinatown*. Chinatown offers a unique blend of old and new, with traditional Chinese goods, modern fashion, and handcrafted items all available in the same area. The *Chinatown Complex* is a great place to start, offering everything from Chinese herbs and medicines to traditional clothing and crafts. If you're looking for souvenirs, *Chinatown Street Market* is filled with stalls selling everything from keychains to intricate tea sets. Chinatown is also home to boutique stores and galleries where you can find more unique, handcrafted items. To explore Chinatown's shopping scene, take the MRT to *Chinatown Station* (North-East Line or Downtown Line).

For travelers looking for a different kind of shopping experience, *Haji Lane* in the Kampong Glam district is perfect for those who appreciate independent boutiques and quirky finds. Haji Lane is known for its narrow streets lined with colorful shops selling everything from handmade jewelry to vintage clothing. It's the ideal place for those who love discovering unique, one-of-a-kind items that you won't find in big shopping malls. Haji Lane is also home to trendy cafés and street art, making it a great place to relax and explore at a slower pace. To get to Haji Lane, take the MRT to *Bugis Station* (East-West Line or Downtown Line), and it's a short walk from there.

For luxury travelers looking for the best in high-end shopping, *The Shoppes at Marina Bay Sands* is a must-visit. Located in the iconic Marina Bay Sands complex, this shopping mall offers a collection of the world's top luxury brands, including Prada, Gucci, and Dior. The Shoppes also features a beautiful setting, with indoor canals and stunning views of Marina Bay.

Beyond shopping, The Shoppes at Marina Bay Sands offers a wide selection of fine dining restaurants and a luxurious cinema experience, making it a complete luxury destination. To get there, take the MRT to *Bayfront Station* (Circle Line or Downtown Line).

If you're interested in buying local products or artisanal goods, *Tiong Bahru Market* and the surrounding area are ideal spots to explore. Tiong Bahru is one of Singapore's oldest residential neighborhoods, but in recent years, it has become a hotspot for boutique shops, artisanal bakeries, and specialty stores. At the *Tiong Bahru Market*, you'll find everything from fresh produce to local snacks and delicacies. The surrounding streets are home to unique stores offering handmade crafts, books, and home décor items. To reach Tiong Bahru, take the MRT to *Tiong Bahru Station* (East-West Line).

Finally, no shopping trip in Singapore would be complete without a visit to *Little India*, one of the city's most colorful and vibrant districts.

Little India is filled with shops selling traditional Indian clothing, spices, jewelry, and home décor. *Mustafa Centre*, a massive 24-hour shopping mall in Little India, is famous for its wide selection of products, ranging from electronics and clothing to food and souvenirs. Shopping in Little India offers a completely different experience from the modern malls, with a focus on traditional goods and a lively market atmosphere. To explore Little India, take the MRT to *Little India Station* (Downtown Line or North-East Line).

However, Singapore offers a shopping experience that caters to all kinds of travelers, from those seeking luxury brands to those hunting for bargains in local markets. Whether you prefer the glitzy malls of Orchard Road or the cultural streets of Chinatown and Little India, there's something for every shopper in Singapore. With its convenient public transport system, getting to these top shopping spots is easy, allowing you to explore the best of what the city has to offer at your own pace.

CHAPTER 17

NIGHTLIFE AND ENTERTAINMENT

Singapore's nightlife is a vibrant and diverse experience, offering a range of options from trendy rooftop bars to cultural performances and lively nightclubs. Whether you're looking for a relaxing evening with spectacular views, live music, or something more high-energy, there's something for everyone to enjoy. Singapore's nightlife also extends beyond drinks and dancing—there are cultural shows, late-night shopping, and even world-class casinos to explore. In this guide, we'll walk through the top nightlife and entertainment spots that travelers should experience while in Singapore, along with helpful tips on how to get there.

For travelers who enjoy sipping cocktails while soaking in breathtaking views, Singapore is home to some of the most stunning *bars and rooftop lounges*. One of the best places to experience this is *Marina Bay Sands SkyPark*, where *Ce La Vi* offers unparalleled views of the city skyline and Marina Bay. This stylish rooftop bar is perfect for those who want to relax with a drink while enjoying the lights of the city from above. Another popular rooftop venue is *1-Altitude*, located at the top of One Raffles Place. As one of the highest alfresco bars in the world, it provides panoramic views of Singapore's skyline, including iconic landmarks such as the Marina Bay Sands and the Singapore Flyer. Both venues are easy to reach by MRT—Marina Bay Sands SkyPark is accessible from *Bayfront Station* (Circle Line or Downtown Line), while 1-Altitude is near *Raffles Place Station* (North-South Line or East-West Line).

For a night filled with energy, *live music venues and nightclubs* are abundant in Singapore, each offering something unique.

Clarke Quay, the riverside nightlife district, is one of the best places to find both live music and nightclubs. A key highlight is *Zouk*, one of Singapore's most famous clubs, offering different rooms with various music genres, from electronic to pop hits. For live music lovers, *Hood Bar & Café* in Bugis is a popular spot known for its lively atmosphere and local bands. This venue is perfect for those who want to enjoy live performances in a more laid-back setting. You can reach Clarke Quay by taking the MRT to *Clarke Quay Station* (North-East Line), and *Hood Bar & Café* is accessible from *Bugis Station* (East-West Line or Downtown Line).

For a more cultural approach to nightlife, Singapore offers numerous *cultural shows and theatre performances* that are perfect for an evening of entertainment. The *Esplanade – Theatres on the Bay* is one of Singapore's top venues for music, dance, and theater performances.

From classical concerts to contemporary theater, Esplanade hosts a variety of shows throughout the year, often featuring both local and international talent. You can also catch free performances at the outdoor theater area, which offers a stunning view of Marina Bay. Another option is the *Singapore Repertory Theatre*, which is known for staging high-quality plays and musicals. Both venues are easily accessible via MRT—*Esplanade Station* (Circle Line) is the closest to the Esplanade, while *Fort Canning Station* (Downtown Line) is nearest to the Singapore Repertory Theatre.

If shopping is your idea of a great night out, Singapore's *late-night shopping and markets* offer plenty of opportunities to explore. *Mustafa Centre* in Little India is one of the best places for late-night shopping, as it's open 24 hours a day. This massive department store sells everything from electronics and clothing to groceries and souvenirs, making it a great stop for night owls.

For a more traditional shopping experience, *Chinatown Street Market* is open until late and offers a wide range of goods, from handcrafted items to delicious street food. It's an excellent spot for travelers who want to explore local culture while picking up some souvenirs. To reach Mustafa Centre, take the MRT to *Farrer Park Station* (North-East Line), and Chinatown Street Market is accessible from *Chinatown Station* (North-East Line or Downtown Line).

For those who enjoy a bit of excitement, Singapore is home to some of the most luxurious *casinos* in Asia. Both the *Marina Bay Sands Casino* and *Resorts World Sentosa Casino* offer a world-class gaming experience with a variety of table games and slot machines. The Marina Bay Sands Casino is set in the heart of the Marina Bay area and offers a more upscale, glamorous gaming atmosphere, while Resorts World Sentosa Casino is located on the lively island of Sentosa, making it a great option if you're looking to combine gaming with other entertainment on the island, such as Universal

Studios or the S.E.A. Aquarium. To get to the Marina Bay Sands Casino, take the MRT to *Bayfront Station* (Circle Line or Downtown Line), and for Resorts World Sentosa Casino, take the MRT to *Harbourfront Station* (North-East Line or Circle Line), then transfer to the Sentosa Express or take a cable car.

If you want to see the best of Singapore's nightlife all in one evening, there are also *nightlife tours* that take you through the city's most popular nightspots. These tours often include stops at rooftop bars, local food markets, and live music venues, giving travelers a full taste of Singapore's diverse entertainment offerings. These tours can be especially helpful for first-time visitors who want to experience a mix of everything in a short amount of time.

However, Singapore's nightlife offers something for every type of traveler.

Whether you're looking for stunning rooftop views, lively music, cultural performances, or exciting casino experiences, the city has a wide array of options to explore after dark. The public transport system, especially the MRT, makes it easy to get to and from these locations, ensuring you can enjoy your night out without worrying about getting around. With its vibrant energy and rich cultural scene, Singapore is sure to offer an unforgettable nightlife experience.

CHAPTER 18

ITINERARY FOR EVERY TRAVELERS

Family-Friendly Itinerary

Day 1:

Start your morning at the *Singapore Zoo*, where kids can enjoy seeing animals in naturalistic habitats. Don't miss the *Rainforest KidzWorld*, which offers animal shows and a water play area.

After lunch, head to *Sentosa Island*. Spend the afternoon at *Universal Studios Singapore*, where the whole family can enjoy thrilling rides and interactive attractions based on popular movies.

End the day at *Siloso Beach*, where kids can relax and play or join in activities like beach volleyball.

Day 2:

In the morning, visit *Gardens by the Bay*. Kids will love the *Flower Dome* and *Cloud Forest*, which are home to unique plants and an indoor waterfall.

In the afternoon, take the *Singapore Flyer*, Asia's largest observation wheel, for stunning views of the city.

For dinner, explore the *Lau Pa Sat* hawker center, where you can try satay and other local dishes.

Day 3:

Start your day at the *S.E.A. Aquarium* on Sentosa Island, where kids can learn about marine life through interactive exhibits.

In the afternoon, visit *Adventure Cove Waterpark* on Sentosa for water slides, a lazy river, and snorkeling with colorful fish.

End the day with the *Wings of Time* show, a stunning display of lights, water, and fire at Sentosa.

Couples Itinerary

Day 1:

Begin with a morning stroll through *Botanic Gardens*, a UNESCO World Heritage Site that offers a peaceful escape with its lush greenery.

Head to *Marina Bay Sands* for lunch and enjoy the view from the *SkyPark* observation deck. Take a romantic walk along the *Helix Bridge* and visit the *ArtScience Museum*.

In the evening, enjoy dinner at *Ce La Vi*, the rooftop bar and restaurant at Marina Bay Sands, with spectacular views of the city skyline.

Day 2:

Start your day with a visit to *Gardens by the Bay* and explore the *Supertree Grove*. For a memorable experience, walk the *OCBC Skyway*, a suspended bridge that offers amazing views of the gardens.

In the afternoon, visit *Chinatown* and discover its rich history. Wander through its colorful streets and temples, and stop at the *Chinatown Heritage Centre*.

End the day with a cruise along the *Singapore River*, enjoying the city's skyline as it lights up at night.

Day 3:

Spend your morning exploring *Sentosa Island*. Visit *Palawan Beach* for a relaxing time or take the cable car ride for beautiful views of the island.

Enjoy lunch at one of the many beachside restaurants before heading to *Tanjong Beach Club* to relax by the water.

In the evening, visit *Clarke Quay*, where you can choose from a variety of waterfront restaurants for a romantic dinner.

Solo Traveler Itinerary

Day 1:

Begin your morning with a visit to *Little India*, where you can explore the vibrant markets, temples, and colorful street art.

For lunch, head to *Tekka Market* and enjoy a traditional Indian meal.

In the afternoon, visit *Chinatown* and explore its historic streets and temples. Make sure to stop by *Sri Mariamman Temple* and *Buddha Tooth Relic Temple*.

End your day at *Gardens by the Bay*, where you can enjoy the *Garden Rhapsody* light and sound show at the *Supertree Grove*.

Day 2:

Start the day with a visit to *Tiong Bahru*, a trendy neighborhood known for its cafes, independent shops, and street art.

After lunch, take a relaxing walk along the *Southern Ridges*, a scenic trail that connects several parks and offers fantastic views of the city.

In the evening, visit *Clarke Quay* to enjoy live music or a casual riverside dinner.

Adventure Seekers Itinerary

Day 1:

Begin your day with a morning hike at *MacRitchie Reservoir* and take the *TreeTop Walk*, a suspension bridge that offers panoramic views of the forest.

In the afternoon, head to *East Coast Park* for some water sports like kayaking, stand-up paddleboarding, or cycling along the coastal trails.

For dinner, visit *East Coast Lagoon Food Village* for some delicious local seafood.

Day 2:

Start with a thrilling experience at *Sentosa's Mega Adventure Park*, where you can try the *MegaZip*, a 450-meter-long zipline with fantastic views of the jungle and beach.

In the afternoon, explore the underwater world at *Adventure Cove Waterpark* and snorkel with colorful fish.

End your day at *Sentosa Beach Bars* to relax and enjoy a drink as the sun sets over the island.

Day 3:

Take a morning kayaking trip with *Kayak Fishing Fever*, where you can combine kayaking with fishing along Singapore's coastline.

In the afternoon, explore *Pulau Ubin*, Singapore's rural island escape, where you can cycle through nature trails and visit the *Chek Jawa Wetlands*.

Return to the mainland for dinner at *Changi Village Hawker Centre*, known for its fresh seafood and local dishes.

Group Travel Itinerary

Day 1:

Start your group adventure with a visit to *Sentosa Island*, where you can enjoy team-based activities like *MegaZip*, and *Wave House*, or try indoor skydiving at *iFly Singapore*.

After a fun morning, have lunch at one of the island's beachside restaurants.

In the afternoon, explore *Universal Studios Singapore* together and enjoy the rides and shows.

End the day with a group dinner at *Clarke Quay*, where you can choose from a variety of restaurants offering different cuisines.

Day 2:

Start your morning with a walking tour of *Chinatown* or *Little India*, exploring the cultural heritage and vibrant streets.

In the afternoon, take a boat cruise on the *Singapore River* and enjoy the sights along Marina Bay.

For your final evening, head to *Marina Bay Sands* for dinner at *Ce La Vi* or one of the other rooftop restaurants, offering breathtaking views of the city.

However, Singapore offers a rich variety of experiences for every type of traveler, from families and couples to solo adventurers and groups. With a well-planned itinerary, you can make the most of your time in this dynamic city, experiencing everything from nature trails and adventure parks to cultural landmarks and modern attractions. Whether you're looking for excitement or relaxation, Singapore has something to offer for everyone.

7-day itinerary

Day 1: Explore Marina Bay and Surroundings

Start your week in Singapore by exploring the iconic Marina Bay area.

Morning: Visit *Marina Bay Sands SkyPark* for a panoramic view of the city. From here, you can see the Marina Bay skyline, the Singapore Flyer, and Gardens by the Bay.

Late Morning: Walk across the *Helix Bridge* and explore the *ArtScience Museum*, where futuristic exhibitions await.

Afternoon: Stroll through *Gardens by the Bay*, one of Singapore's most famous attractions. Don't miss the *Flower Dome* and *Cloud Forest*, and take a walk on the *OCBC Skyway* for a closer look at the Supertrees.

Evening: End your day with the *Spectra Light and Water Show* at Marina Bay Sands, then have dinner at the *Ce La Vi* rooftop restaurant.

Day 2: Sentosa Island

Dedicate a full day to Sentosa Island for fun and relaxation.

Morning: Start your day at *Universal Studios Singapore* and enjoy thrilling rides and shows based on popular movies.

Afternoon: Visit the *S.E.A. Aquarium* to explore the underwater world and get close to marine life.

Late Afternoon: Relax on *Siloso Beach* or *Palawan Beach*. If you're adventurous, try *MegaZip* or indoor skydiving at *iFly Singapore*.

Evening: Enjoy the *Wings of Time* show on the beach and have dinner at one of the many beachside restaurants.

Day 3: Cultural and Historical Exploration

Immerse yourself in Singapore's rich history and diverse cultures.

Morning: Visit *Chinatown* and start with the *Chinatown Heritage Centre* to learn about the early Chinese settlers in Singapore. Explore the *Sri Mariamman Temple* and *Buddha Tooth Relic Temple*.

Afternoon: Head to *Little India* to experience another side of Singapore's cultural diversity. Visit *Sri Veeramakaliamman Temple* and shop for souvenirs at *Tekka Market*.

Evening: End your day in the *Kampong Glam* district, where you can visit the *Sultan Mosque* and stroll through *Haji Lane* for independent boutiques and vibrant street art. Enjoy dinner at a nearby café.

Day 4: Nature and Outdoor Adventure

Enjoy Singapore's green spaces and outdoor activities.

Morning: Begin with a visit to the *Singapore Botanic Gardens*, a UNESCO World Heritage Site. Don't miss the *National Orchid Garden*.

Afternoon: Take a walk along the *Southern Ridges*, a 10-kilometer trail that connects parks and offers stunning views of the city's natural and urban landscapes. The *Henderson Waves* bridge is a highlight.

Evening: For dinner, head to the *Dempsey Hill* area, where you'll find several upscale restaurants in a tranquil, garden-like setting.

Day 5: Adventure and Wildlife

Experience Singapore's more adventurous side and discover its wildlife.

Morning: Start with a hike at *MacRitchie Reservoir* and experience the *TreeTop Walk*, a suspension bridge that offers views of the surrounding forest.

Afternoon: Visit the *Singapore Zoo* and take the *River Safari* to see a wide range of animals, including pandas and manatees.

Evening: In the evening, enjoy the unique experience of the *Night Safari*, the world's first nocturnal wildlife park, where you can see animals in their natural nighttime environments.

Day 6: Shopping and Leisure

Take a break from sightseeing and enjoy some shopping and leisure activities.

Morning: Begin your shopping journey at *Orchard Road*, Singapore's main shopping street, where you'll find luxury malls like *ION Orchard* and more affordable options like *Far East Plaza*.

Afternoon: Continue shopping or visit *Bugis Street Market* for souvenirs, clothing, and accessories at more affordable prices. Alternatively, head to *Haji Lane* for independent boutiques.

Evening: End the day with dinner at *Clarke Quay*, where you can enjoy riverside dining followed by a relaxing *Singapore River Cruise*.

Day 7: Day Trip to Pulau Ubin and Changi Village

Take a step back in time and explore one of Singapore's last rustic villages.

Morning: Take a boat ride from *Changi Point Ferry Terminal* to *Pulau Ubin*, a small island that offers a glimpse of Singapore's past. Rent a bike and explore the island, visit the *Chek Jawa Wetlands*, and enjoy the quiet, natural environment.

Afternoon: After returning to the mainland, explore *Changi Village*. Visit *Changi Beach Park* for a relaxing walk, and enjoy some local dishes at *Changi Village Hawker Centre*.

Evening: Return to the city and spend your last night at *Marina Bay Sands*, enjoying a meal with a view or visiting the *Marina Barrage* for one last view of the stunning city skyline.

This 7-day itinerary gives you a comprehensive experience of Singapore, blending its modern attractions with its rich history, cultural diversity, and green spaces. Whether you're into shopping, outdoor adventure, or exploring unique attractions, this itinerary will ensure you get the most out of your visit.

CHAPTER 19

TOUR GUIDES AND OPERATORS

Tour guides and operators play a key role in helping travelers make the most of their trip to Singapore, whether you're visiting for the first time or looking to discover hidden gems that are off the beaten path. With a wide range of tours available—ranging from private guided tours to budget-friendly group options—there is something for every type of traveler. Choosing the right tour guide or operator can enhance your experience by providing insights into Singapore's history, culture, and attractions that you may not otherwise get from exploring on your own. This guide will give you a detailed look at the different types of tours available, as well as tips for selecting the best tour operators for your specific needs.

For those seeking a more personalized experience, *top-rated private tour guides* offer a tailored way to explore Singapore.

Private guides provide a one-on-one experience and can customize the tour to suit your preferences, whether you're interested in cultural landmarks, local cuisine, or natural attractions. These guides are often highly knowledgeable about the city and can give you deep insights into its history, traditions, and local life. A popular choice among visitors is *Jane's Singapore Tours*, which specializes in walking tours through historical districts, hidden neighborhoods, and nature trails. With a private guide, you have the flexibility to set your own pace and explore the areas that interest you the most. To find a top-rated guide, it's best to look for recommendations on travel platforms or check reviews on sites like TripAdvisor or Viator.

For travelers on a budget, *group tour operators* offer a cost-effective way to explore Singapore while still benefiting from the expertise of a guide. Group tours are a great option if you're looking to see the main sights while meeting other travelers.

One well-known operator is *Big Bus Tours*, which offers hop-on, hop-off bus tours around Singapore's top attractions, such as Marina Bay, Gardens by the Bay, and Orchard Road. These tours allow you to cover a lot of ground at an affordable price, and you can hop off at any stop to explore further before catching the next bus. Another option is *Duck Tours*, a unique land-and-water sightseeing experience that takes you through Singapore's city streets and into Marina Bay on a modified amphibious vehicle. Group tours provide convenience, and the guides often share fun facts and stories about the places you visit, making it an easy way to learn about the city.

For families, solo travelers, and couples looking for something a little more specialized, there are many operators that offer *customized tours*. These tours are designed to cater to your specific interests, whether you're traveling as a family with young children, a solo traveler looking to explore Singapore's hidden gems, or a couple seeking romantic experiences.

For families, *Hello Singapore Tours* offers kid-friendly tours that include attractions like the Singapore Zoo, Sentosa Island, and the ArtScience Museum. These tours are structured to keep children engaged while allowing parents to enjoy the sights as well. Solo travelers might enjoy *Monster Day Tours*, which offers offbeat itineraries such as food tours, street art walks, and even hidden nature spots that most tourists miss. For couples, private sunset cruises or walking tours through historical neighborhoods like Kampong Glam can be arranged to provide a more intimate experience. Customized tours allow you to create your ideal itinerary, ensuring that you see the parts of Singapore that most appeal to you.

If you're an outdoor enthusiast, Singapore has plenty to offer in terms of adventure, and there are several *adventure tour operators* that can help you make the most of the city's natural surroundings.

For example, *Kayak Fishing Fever* offers guided kayaking and fishing tours in the waters around Singapore, giving you a chance to explore the island's coastline from a unique perspective. Another option is *Bike Around Tour Singapore*, which provides bike tours that take you through some of the city's most scenic and culturally rich neighborhoods, including Little India and the Civic District. For those looking for hiking adventures, *The Travel Intern* offers tours that guide you through Singapore's nature reserves, including the Southern Ridges and MacRitchie Reservoir. These tours are great for travelers who enjoy being active and want to explore Singapore's outdoor offerings.

When selecting a tour operator in Singapore, it's important to consider a few key factors to ensure you have the best experience possible. First, check the operator's reputation by reading reviews from previous travelers. Sites like TripAdvisor or Google Reviews can provide helpful insights into the quality of the tours and the professionalism of the guides.

Second, consider the type of experience you're looking for—whether you prefer a more personalized private tour, a budget-friendly group tour, or a specialized adventure tour, some operators cater to each style of travel. Third, inquire about what's included in the tour. Some operators may provide extra services like transportation, meals, or entrance tickets to attractions, while others may charge separately for these. Lastly, ensure that the tour matches your schedule and interests. Some tours may be more comprehensive and take a full day, while others may offer half-day or shorter options if you have limited time.

Lastly, Singapore has a wide variety of tour guides and operators that cater to all kinds of travelers. Whether you're looking for a personalized private tour, a budget-friendly group experience, or an adventurous outdoor excursion, there's an option to suit your needs.

By choosing the right tour operator, you can enhance your visit to Singapore, gaining deeper insights into the city while ensuring you make the most of your time. With many highly rated operators available, it's easy to find the perfect tour for your trip to Singapore.

TOURIST TRAPS TO AVOID

While Singapore is a very safe and welcoming destination, like any popular tourist spot, it has a few places and situations where travelers might end up spending more than expected or miss out on a more authentic experience. Avoiding these common tourist traps will help you make the most of your time and budget, allowing you to experience the true essence of Singapore.

One of the most common tourist traps in Singapore is overpaying for souvenirs, especially around major attractions.

Shops near Marina Bay Sands, Sentosa, and other popular sites often charge significantly more for basic items like magnets, keychains, and T-shirts.

Instead, try shopping in areas like Chinatown or Bugis Street, where you can find similar souvenirs at more reasonable prices. Bugis Street Market, in particular, is known for its affordable goods, and Chinatown offers a broader variety with more local flair.

Another common pitfall is the *Singapore River Cruise*. While the boat ride provides nice views of Marina Bay Sands, Clarke Quay, and the city skyline, some find the ticket prices a bit high for the experience. As an alternative, you can get similar scenic views from the Singapore Flyer or simply stroll along the riverbank at Marina Bay, which is free and offers plenty of great photo opportunities.

In food and dining, the popular hawker centers are an incredible part of Singapore's food culture, but tourists can sometimes end up paying inflated prices at stalls that cater mainly to tourists.

At places like Lau Pa Sat, stalls may increase prices on popular items during peak hours.

Instead, try visiting local-frequented hawker centers like Maxwell Food Centre, Old Airport Road Food Centre, or Tiong Bahru Market. These places offer an authentic dining experience with lower prices, allowing you to sample Singapore's famous dishes without overspending.

When visiting *Sentosa Island*, be aware that certain attractions and experiences may come with additional costs that aren't always necessary to enjoy the island. The Sentosa Express and the Cable Car are both popular ways to reach the island, but the Sentosa Boardwalk is free and offers a pleasant, scenic walk over to Sentosa. Once on the island, some activities like beaches and nature trails are free to enjoy, so be sure to check what's included before purchasing expensive day passes.

Another trap to avoid is the temptation to visit high-end malls for shopping.

While places like Orchard Road, Marina Bay Sands, and ION Orchard offer luxury shopping, these areas are typically geared towards high-end brands.

Unless you're specifically looking for designer items, shopping at smaller boutiques, local markets, or shopping complexes like Bugis Junction can offer more unique finds at affordable prices.

Trick taxi fares can also be an issue in some tourist areas. Although Singapore is known for its fair and regulated taxis, it's best to avoid taxis that don't use a meter or those offering "special rates." Always check that the meter is on before starting your trip, or consider using a ride-hailing app like Grab for more transparency.

Finally, some tourists fall into the trap of expensive spa and massage centers targeted at visitors, especially in high-end malls or hotel areas. Prices at these locations can be very high, so consider exploring local spa chains or neighborhood massage centers for a more reasonably priced experience.

Local options often provide excellent service at a fraction of the cost, allowing you to relax without breaking the bank.

By keeping these tips in mind, you can navigate around common tourist traps and enjoy a more genuine and affordable experience in Singapore. This way, you'll have more to spend on the true highlights and hidden gems that make Singapore such a fascinating destination.

CHAPTER 20

ADDITIONAL RESOURCES

Preparing for a trip to Singapore requires the right resources to ensure your experience is smooth, enjoyable, and well-organized. With helpful travel apps, knowledge of the local currency, and key information about what to pack, you'll be ready for a memorable journey. These essential tips will provide you with practical advice for navigating Singapore, understanding its climate, managing your budget, and staying safe. Here's a comprehensive collection of resources and information that every traveler should know before visiting this vibrant city.

Best Travel Apps for Your Trip

Having the right apps on your smartphone can simplify navigation, help you find local spots, and even assist with language.

Here are some must-have travel apps for Singapore:

Google Maps: This is essential for getting around. It provides accurate directions for walking, driving, or using public transportation. Public transport routes are well integrated, making it easy to find bus or MRT stations and routes.

Grab: Grab is the main ride-hailing app in Singapore, similar to Uber. Use it to book taxis or private cars for convenient transport across the city.

SG MRT: This app provides detailed information about Singapore's MRT system, including maps, schedules, and the quickest routes between stations.

iTranslate or Google Translate: While English is widely spoken, having a translation app can be helpful if you want to explore local phrases or if you find yourself in areas where other languages are used.

Visit Singapore Travel Guide: This official tourism app offers comprehensive guides on attractions, events, and itineraries, helping you make the most of your time in Singapore.

Currency, ATMs, and Budgeting Tips

Understanding the currency and managing your budget will help you enjoy Singapore without overspending.

Currency: The official currency is the Singapore Dollar (SGD), often referred to as "dollars" or simply "S$". Notes and coins are widely used, and ATMs are available throughout the city.

ATMs: ATMs are found in airports, shopping centers, and MRT stations. They accept major cards like Visa, Mastercard, and American Express. Most ATMs allow withdrawals in Singapore dollars, with fees depending on your bank.

Credit and Debit Cards: Credit cards are widely accepted in Singapore, especially in hotels, restaurants, and stores.

However, some hawker centers and smaller shops may only accept cash, so it's wise to carry some cash for these situations.

Budgeting: Singapore is known for being relatively expensive. Street food at hawker centers is very affordable and delicious, while upscale dining can be pricey. The MRT and buses are economical ways to get around, while taxis and ride-hailing services are more costly but convenient.

Emergency Contacts and Safety Information

Being familiar with emergency contacts and safety information will give you peace of mind during your trip.

Emergency Numbers: Dial 999 for police, 995 for the fire department and medical emergencies, and 1777 for non-emergency ambulance services.

Hospitals: Singapore's healthcare system is one of the best in the world. Public hospitals like *Singapore General Hospital* and private options like *Mount Elizabeth Hospital* provide high-quality services.

Safety: Singapore is one of the safest cities globally, with strict laws and low crime rates. However, it's always wise to take precautions, such as safeguarding your belongings and being aware of your surroundings in crowded areas.

Travel Insurance: While Singapore is safe, it's still a good idea to have travel insurance that covers health, accidents, and theft. This will provide coverage in case of medical emergencies or loss of personal items.

Weather and Climate: What to Expect and How to Pack

Singapore's climate is tropical, with high humidity, consistent warmth, and periodic rain showers.

Temperature: Average temperatures range from 25°C to 31°C (77°F to 88°F) throughout the year.

Humidity: Humidity is generally high, around 70-80%, making the weather feel warmer. Dressing in breathable clothing is recommended.

Rainy Season: Rainfall is common year-round, with two main monsoon periods. The Northeast Monsoon (December to March) brings heavier rainfall, while the Southwest Monsoon (June to September) has shorter, more frequent showers.

Packing Tips: Given the tropical climate, pack clothes that are suitable for warm, humid weather and rain. Lightweight fabrics, umbrellas, and comfortable walking shoes are essential. A rain jacket or poncho is useful for quick cover during sudden showers, and sunscreen is important for sun protection on bright days.

These resources will help you feel prepared and informed for your trip to Singapore.

From packing essentials to navigating the city with helpful apps, having this knowledge will ensure that your travel experience is enjoyable, safe, and smooth.

With practical tools at your fingertips and a clear understanding of what to expect, you can focus on exploring Singapore's attractions and soaking in its vibrant culture.

CONCLUSION

As you conclude your journey through this travel guide, you should now have a detailed understanding of all that Singapore has to offer, from world-renowned attractions to the lesser-known gems waiting to be explored. Singapore is a city that truly offers a rich experience for every traveler, with each neighborhood, landmark, and cultural site bringing its unique perspective on the city's heritage and modern identity.

Singapore's blend of cultures and traditions sets it apart, providing visitors with an immersive experience in a place where Malay, Chinese, Indian, and Western influences come together. From the vibrant streets of Chinatown, Little India, and Kampong Glam to the sleek architecture of Marina Bay Sands and the futuristic Gardens by the Bay, Singapore embodies a harmonious mix of the old and the new.

These contrasts are what makes Singapore such a fascinating city to explore—whether you're walking down the historic streets or admiring the cityscape from a rooftop bar, there's always something unexpected around the corner.

Traveling in Singapore is made easy by its well-organized transport system, allowing you to move effortlessly from one attraction to another. The MRT, buses, and pedestrian-friendly streets enable you to cover a lot in a day without the stress of complex travel arrangements. With a variety of accommodation options, from luxurious hotels to budget-friendly hostels, the city accommodates all types of travelers comfortably. The diverse food scene, ranging from award-winning restaurants to local hawker centers, allows you to explore the tastes of Singapore affordably and conveniently.

For families, solo travelers, couples, and adventure-seekers, Singapore's wide range of attractions provides something unique for each kind of traveler.

Families can explore attractions like the Singapore Zoo and Sentosa Island, offering safe and engaging activities for children. Couples have endless choices for romantic evenings, from sunset cruises along the Singapore River to cozy dinners at top-rated restaurants. Adventure enthusiasts can venture out to Pulau Ubin, kayak along East Coast Park, or hike through the Southern Ridges, experiencing the natural side of the city. Solo travelers, too, will find plenty of welcoming spaces, unique experiences, and opportunities to learn about the city's history and culture.

Practical travel tips, like currency information, essential packing advice, and helpful travel apps, add convenience to your journey, ensuring you're well-prepared to explore. Knowing what to expect in terms of weather, safety, and transportation will help you feel more confident as you travel, leaving you free to enjoy each day to the fullest.

In summary, Singapore is more than just a stopover or a short visit—it's a destination worth exploring in depth. The city offers a journey that goes beyond sightseeing, inviting you to take part in its lively festivals, taste its multicultural cuisine, connect with its locals, and explore its diverse landscapes. With this guide in hand, you're ready to uncover all that Singapore has to offer, equipped with practical knowledge, insider tips, and a curated list of must-see attractions and hidden spots that will make your experience unforgettable.

May your time in Singapore be filled with discovery, excitement, and meaningful memories. Safe travels and enjoy every moment of your Singapore adventure!

SINGAPORE TRAVEL JOURNAL (BONUS)

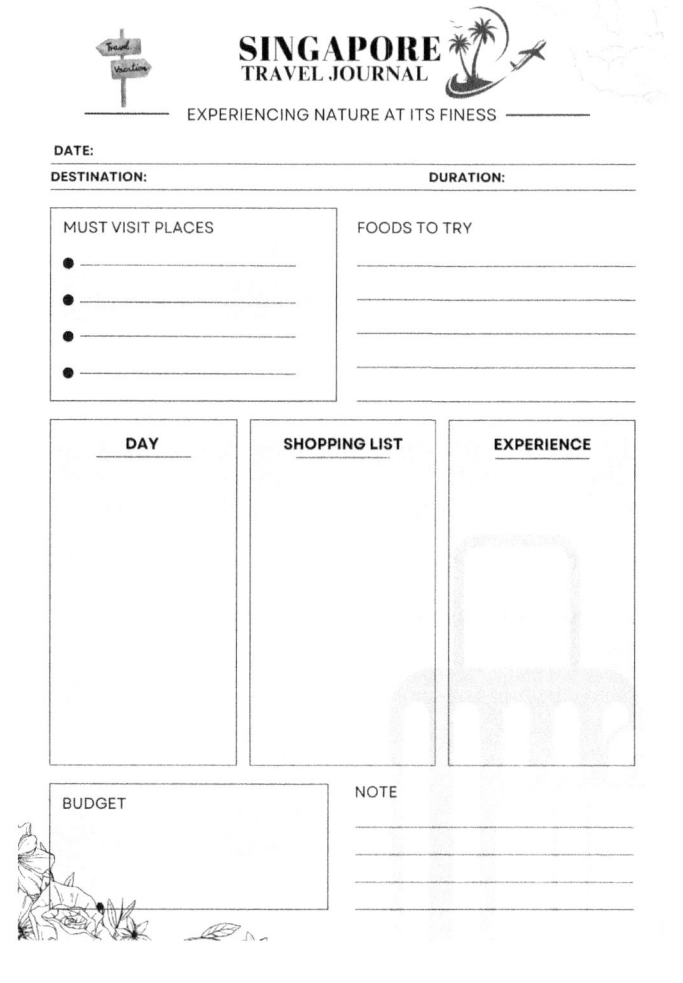

SINGAPORE TRAVEL JOURNAL

EXPERIENCING NATURE AT ITS FINESS

DATE:

DESTINATION: **DURATION:**

MUST VISIT PLACES

-
-
-
-

FOODS TO TRY

DAY

SHOPPING LIST

EXPERIENCE

BUDGET

NOTE

SINGAPORE BUCKET LIST

SINGAPORE
TRAVEL JOURNAL
EXPERIENCING NATURE AT ITS FINESS

DATE:
DESTINATION: **DURATION:**

MUST VISIT PLACES	FOODS TO TRY
•	
•	
•	
•	

DAY	SHOPPING LIST	EXPERIENCE

BUDGET	NOTE

SINGAPORE BUCKET LIST

SINGAPORE
TRAVEL JOURNAL
EXPERIENCING NATURE AT ITS FINESS

DATE:
DESTINATION: **DURATION:**

MUST VISIT PLACES
-
-
-
-

FOODS TO TRY

DAY

SHOPPING LIST

EXPERIENCE

BUDGET

NOTE

SINGAPORE BUCKET LIST

SINGAPORE
TRAVEL JOURNAL
EXPERIENCING NATURE AT ITS FINESS

DATE:

DESTINATION: **DURATION:**

MUST VISIT PLACES
-
-
-
-

FOODS TO TRY

DAY

SHOPPING LIST

EXPERIENCE

BUDGET

NOTE

SINGAPORE BUCKET LIST

SINGAPORE TRAVEL JOURNAL
EXPERIENCING NATURE AT ITS FINESS

DATE:
DESTINATION: **DURATION:**

MUST VISIT PLACES
-
-
-
-

FOODS TO TRY

DAY

SHOPPING LIST

EXPERIENCE

BUDGET

NOTE

SINGAPORE BUCKET LIST

SINGAPORE
TRAVEL JOURNAL
EXPERIENCING NATURE AT ITS FINESS

DATE:

DESTINATION: **DURATION:**

MUST VISIT PLACES
- _____
- _____
- _____
- _____

FOODS TO TRY

DAY | **SHOPPING LIST** | **EXPERIENCE**

BUDGET | **NOTE**

SINGAPORE BUCKET LIST

SINGAPORE TRAVEL JOURNAL
EXPERIENCING NATURE AT ITS FINESS

DATE:

DESTINATION: **DURATION:**

MUST VISIT PLACES
-
-
-
-

FOODS TO TRY

DAY

SHOPPING LIST

EXPERIENCE

BUDGET

NOTE

Printed in Great Britain
by Amazon